Reflections

Second Edition

John Dennis
San Francisco State University

Suzanne Griffin
South Seattle Community College

Heinle & Heinle Publishers
A Division of Wadsworth, Inc.
Boston, MA 02116 U.S. A.

The publication of *Reflections*, Second Edition was directed by the members of the Newbury House Publishing Team at Heinle & Heinle:

Erik Gundersen, Editorial Director
Gabrielle B. McDonald, Production Editor

Also participating in the publication of this textbook were:

Publisher: Stanley J. Galek
Editorial Production Manager: Elizabeth Holthaus
Project Manager: Woodshed Productions
Assistant Editor: Karen P. Hazar
Associate Marketing Manager: Donna Hamilton
Production Assistant: Maryellen Eschmann
Manufacturing Coordinator: Martha Leibs-Heckly
Interior Designer: Barbara Goodchild
Cover Illustrator and Designer: Lisa Desimini

Heinle & Heinle Publishers is a division of Wadsworth, Inc.

Manufactured in the United States of America

Photograph and Text Credits appear on page 232, which constitutes a part of this copyright page.

Library of Congress Cataloging-in-Publication Data
Dennis, John. 1920 –
  Reflections / John Dennis & Suzanne Griffin. — 2nd ed.
      p.   cm.
  Rev. ed. of: Reflections, an intermediate reader / Suzanne Griffin, John Dennis. Rowley, Mass. : Newbury House Publishers, c1979.
  ISBN 0-8384-4846-1
  1. English language — Textbooks for foreign speakers. 2. Readers.
I. Griffin, Suzanne M., 1945 – . II. Griffin, Suzanne M., 1945 – .
Reflections, an intermediate reader. III. Title.
PE1128.D39 1994
428.6'4 — dc20   93-47459
                                                                  CIP

ISBN: 0-8384-4846-1
10 9 8 7 6 5 4 3 2

Contents

About This Book

Reflections is a graded, intermediate level reading text for learners of English who are studying this language in either an English speaking or a non-English speaking environment. A central goal of this text is to provide intermediate-level students with access to the richness and diversity of literature within the English language. Toward this end, this second edition of *Reflections*, like its predecessor, is composed of literary selections. The ideas and issues in these selections are being read and discussed by young adult readers in North America.

With guidance and insight provided by teachers throughout the ESL/EFL community, readings have been grouped under five themes: conventional wisdom (*Unit 1: Fables*), personal sorrows (*Unit 2: Sorrows*), memories from youth (*Unit 3: Memories*), relationships (*Unit 4: Ties*), and visions of the future (*Unit 5: Visions*). Most selections are presented exactly as they were originally written. A few are shortened and occasionally language has been edited to ensure that the writing is comprehensible to non-native speakers of English.

The thoughts and feelings of writers from different times and places are reflected in their work. Exercises that precede and follow each reading encourage learners to think about and study patriotism, social responsibility, racial prejudice, personal relationships, and self-discovery. Eventually, what students learn from these activities will find its way into their thinking and self-expression.

How To Use This Book

Although this text can be used for self-instruction or tutorial instruction, it will be most effectively used in a group setting. The questions and activities in "Sharing Experiences" are designed to draw upon the collective experiences of the learners to build the context (i.e., schema) for understanding the reading. Learners will expand their English vocabulary around topics in the readings by sharing and comparing ideas as they respond to discussion questions following each reading.

Individuals who use the text for self-instruction will be able to check their answers against those in the answer key for items which call for specific responses (primarily exercises A-C and E). Responses to cues which allow for a variety of answers (Sharing Experiences and post-reading Exercises D and F) can be checked by referring to the text of the reading or by consulting with a person who is proficient in English.

Pre-reading activities
These activities intend to enable students to develop contexts (schemata); that is, to help students to "read themselves" as they read various writers. Questions and multi-sensory activities in *Sharing Experiences*

elicit learners' knowledge and experiences which will enhance their understanding of the theme, subject and mood of the reading. In addition, information about each writer and reading gives learners the social and historical context of the work, as well as an insight into the writer's purpose.

The reading process

Prior to actually reading the text, learners should **survey the entire reading**, looking at the photographs, the first line of each paragraph, and the glossed words on each page. After this overview, the learners should look over the items in **Exercise A**. After reviewing the information requested, learners should read rapidly with the purpose of **gathering information**. Learners can check their responses in Exercise A against the answer key. Discussion of answers which differ from those in the answer key is encouraged. Learners should present evidence and arguments for their answers.

Learners should read the statement or question in **Part One of Exercise B** before a quick **second reading** of the selection to understand the main idea. **Part Two of Exercise B** helps learners determine the sequence of events in the reading and identify whomever is performing each action. A careful **third reading** is necessary to respond to the items in Part Two of this exercise. Learners will also have to review glossed words in order to complete some items.

After three readings, learners should be able to successfully complete **Exercise C**, which requires them to interpret and analyze the ideas in the selection.

Vocabulary, structure, and style

These exercises vary in focus and length because they are tied directly to the language and syntax of the story. Some **Word Study** exercises extend learners' vocabulary by using synonyms, antonyms and analogies to help them understand meaning. Other exercises focus on word formation (prefixes, suffixes, and roots) and show how grammatical function changes the form of the words. **Structure exercises** draw learners'attention to the syntactical features of the reading and give them new contexts in which to use these structures. Exercises on **style** focus on the techniques used by the author to convey meaning, mood, and point of view. Learners are asked to analyze the author's diction, use of imagery or rhetoric in order to better understand *what* the author is saying, as well as *how* he/she has chosen to communicate the message.

Discussion and writing questions

This exercise is designed to help learners think critically about the ideas in the text and to extend these ideas into situations which are familiar to them. Responses to the questions and statements in the exercise may be either oral or written. More learners are likely to volunteer oral responses to the discussion questions if they work on this exercise in small groups rather than in a large class setting. Individuals in each group can take turns answering the questions, asking follow up questions for clarification, recording the answers of their classmates, and reporting the response of their group to other groups in the class.

Many of the discussion questions call upon learners to find additional information on the topic and to share the information with others in the class. Other items in this exercise encourage students to perform a task or engage in a role play activity related to a situation in the reading. Such activities help students understand that reading is not a passive activity. Reading can and should lead to active involvement in a subject.

Surely, one of these activities is writing. The **Discussion Questions** are designed to prepare students for self-expression — either oral or written. The written responses may take several forms. **1)** The completion of a dialogue (see "Thank You Ma'm" and "You Go Your Way, I'll Go Mine") **2)** The creation of a passage, by definition a unified (topical) piece of writing of unspecified length. It is not a formal contraption with paragraphs and transitions and topic sentences. A passage is a fragment, written in response to some kind of impulse or provocation. As such, it can be a pretty reliable indication of what students are thinking and how well they can transfer their thoughts to the page. The exercise called **Additional Activities** frequently contains proposals for writing described in **1** and **2** above.

Summary of reading skills

The sequence of activities preceding and following each reading selection suggests strategies for learners reading other texts in English. Learners should begin by trying to relate something in their own experience to the text. Next, they should find out what they can about the content and rationale for the text by learning about the author, looking at illustrations, and reviewing the historical and social setting of the text. Through several successive readings, students should be able to extract critical information from the reading, sequence events, understand the main idea, and interpret the information presented.

Through further analysis, learners will be able to distinguish the author's point of view or intention by focusing on the selection of vocabulary, structure, and style. Understanding of the art of relating language and syntax to the purpose of each reading should ultimately lead learners to an appreciation of English literature produced by accomplished writers in contrast to mediocre writing that frequently characterizes popular periodicals and texts.

1

Fables Old and New

Do you know what fables are? Fables are very short stories whose purpose is to show people better ways to think about their actions. Sometimes fables teach people lessons in morality: how to be good people. Other times fables teach people to avoid foolish mistakes: how to be sensible and practical. Usually fables end with a *moral*: one or two lines that express the teaching in the fable.

Fables have been part of every culture since the earliest times. These stories were told and heard long before they were written and read. Old fables use animals that act and speak like people. Modern fables or fables changed (adapted) from old fables mix animals and people together. You will find both old and new fables in this unit.

LESSON 1

The Donkey in the Lion's Skin

The Writer

AESOP

Aesop is a mysterious person. Perhaps he lived and died in Greece some five hundred years before the birth of Christ. Aesop is said to have died violently. His sharp wit and his unkind remarks about others may have led to his death. Our uncertainty about Aesop's life has made some scholars doubt his existence completely.

But *someone* named Aesop went about telling fables in Greece. They were oral poems at first, and then they became written prose tales. About one hundred tales were translated from Greek into Latin; later they were translated into other European languages. Different cultures surely changed the settings and the characters in Aesop's fables.

The Reading

Aesop's fables always use animals to tell their stories; sometimes the fables use human characters as well. Both animals and humans appear in the two fables here. Whether the characters in a fable are animals or humans, they have a weakness or a temptation that gets them into trouble.

Fables use simple language, but the kind of wisdom they present to us is not simple or easy to practice.

SHARING EXPERIENCES

Compare your responses with those of your classmates. (You may need your dictionary for this exercise.)

❏ Which animals make these sounds? *Bray, roar, shriek, squeal, bark, purr, moo, bellow, chirp, quack.* Make a list of animals and the sounds they make.

❏ Describe how each animal moves. Which animals can do the following: *run, lumber, rear, kick their heels, wave their forelegs, fall, crouch, jump, spring, fly*?

❏ When and why do people wear costumes? Have you ever worn a costume? When/Why? How did you feel while wearing the costume? Did you fool very many people?

❏ Does your language have a saying like this one: "He who pretends to be something he is not will always, sooner or later, give away the truth"?

The Donkey in the Lion's Skin

Adapted from Aesop

A Donkey once found a Lion's skin which had been left out in the sun to dry.

2   "Aha!" he said to himself, "It will be more fun to make believe I'm a Lion than to go around as a Donkey."

3   So he dressed himself up in the Lion's skin and went back toward the village where he lived. Soon on the country roads he began to meet the people of the town. Seeing him come *lumbering* toward them, they thought him truly a Lion, and all ran away from him as fast as their legs could go. Some were

---

lumbering — walking slowly and heavily

carrying great bundles on their heads, but they turned around and ran, their bundles falling this way and that. Some were driving wagons or carts, but they sprang to the ground with a shriek, left everything and *fled*. Then the oxen and horses reared up in the air, waving their front legs wildly, turned around and ran away, too, with the wagons tipping and tilting behind them. Men, women, children, dogs, horses, cats, oxen, sheep and even the pigs all kicked up their heels and fell over each other! Shrieking, barking, bellowing, squealing, they ran up the dusty road!

4   The donkey had a fine time that day. He crouched like a Lion, he sprang, he chased! What sport he was having! He almost thought he was really a Lion. But at last, wishing to seem even more like the King of Beasts, he said to himself:

5   "I'll roar, and I'll roar, and I'll roar! Then they'll think I'm the fiercest Lion that ever came out of the Forest. I'll have my own way in the village and drive men and beasts wherever I choose."

6   So he lifted up his voice with all its strength, but alas! Instead of roaring, he let out a loud, *ridiculous bray*! "Ee-aw! Ee-aw! Ee-aw!"

7   The people stopped running away at once.

8   "Why! he's only a donkey in a Lion's skin!" they cried, and they picked up sticks and ran after him. Then it was his turn to kick up his heels and run! But it was useless. He could not get away. The people whom he had tricked caught him and held him, using their sticks on his back until his master came up. Then his master turned him out of the lion's skin immediately and, amid the laughter of the crowd, led him back to his proper business of carrying loads.

9   Shortly afterwards a Fox came up to the Donkey and said, "Ah, you gave away the secret of who you were by your voice. He who pretends to be something he is not, will always, sooner or later, give away the truth."

---

fled — ran away (from the verb flee)
ridiculous bray — foolish, silly sound

EXERCISES

Exercise A: Recalling the Reading

Read each statement below and decide whether it is *true* or *false*. If the statement is false, correct it to make a true statement.

1. This fable took place in a city.
2. The Donkey found the Lion's skin.
3. The Donkey amused the villagers at first.
4. The Donkey wanted to be powerful like a real Lion.
5. When the Donkey brayed "Ee-aw! Ee-aw!" the villagers were frightened and fled.
6. The villagers caught the Donkey and beat him with sticks.
7. The Donkey's master sold him to the zoo.
8. The moral of the fable is spoken by a Fox.

Exercise B: Understanding the Reading

Summarize the main idea.

1. Quickly read the entire story again. In one sentence, tell your classmates what happened to the donkey.

2. Identify the person(s) or thing(s) referred to in each phrase. Pay special attention to the words in **boldface**.

    the villagers   the donkey
    a. ". . . ~~they~~ thought ~~him~~ truly a Lion."
    b. ". . . reared up in the air, waving **their** forelegs wildly . . ."
    c. ". . . kicked up **their** heels and fell over each other!"
    d. ". . . **he** sprang, **he** chased!"
    e. "**I'll** have my own way in the village . . ."
    f. "**He** could not get away."
    g. ". . . led him back to his proper business of carrying loads."
    h. ". . . came up to the Donkey and said, 'Ah, you gave away the secret of who you were by your voice. . . .' "

Exercise C: Analyzing Ideas

Choose the correct statements to complete the sentences below. You may have more than one answer for some sentences.

1. The Donkey wanted to become a Lion because
   a. a Lion is the King of Beasts.
   b. Lions are fierce and powerful.
   c. the Donkey didn't like his master.

2. The villagers ran from the Donkey in the Lion's skin because
   a. they couldn't see very well.
   b. they weren't very intelligent.
   c. they truly believed he was a Lion.

3. The best nouns to describe the villagers' actions when they saw the Donkey in the Lion's skin are
   a. pleasure.   d. flee.
   b. fright.   e. tricky.
   c. panic.   f. amusement.

4. The villagers discovered the Donkey in the Lion's skin when
   a. he brayed "Ee-aw!"
   b. he kicked up his heels.
   c. his master took off the Lion's skin.

5. Another way of telling the moral of this fable is:
   a. Don't say anything and you won't get into trouble.
   b. Don't try to change yourself.
   c. Don't pretend to be someone you cannot be.
   d. Stay away from villagers with sticks.
   e. Don't try to live in someone else's skin.

Exercise D: Word Study: Part One

Two = word Verbs: verb + *away*

1. "The Donkey in the Lion's Skin" uses three different verbs followed by *away*. Which verbs are they?
2. Words that follow verbs are called "adverbs," "particles" (words that don't change their form), or sometimes "prepositions." We are calling these verb + particle combinations *two-word verbs*. When the verb adds this particle, the meaning of the verb changes:
   i. get + away = escape
   ii. get + up = arise or stand
   iii. get + out = leave
3. You know what *run* means. When you add *away*, how does the meaning change?
4. When the Fox tells the Donkey, "He . . . will always *give away* the truth," how is *give away* different from the verb *give*?
5. How do these verbs change their meanings when they add *away*?
   a. "*Go* away. I can't talk to you now."
   b. She is not here. She *is* away on a trip.
   c. Please don't *turn* away. Look at me.
   d. *Come* away. We've waited long enough.
   e. Shall I *carry* it away or leave it here?

Exercise D: Word Study: Part Two

Verbs + *ing*

1. When we add -*ing* to verbs, we change both their *form* (carry → carrying) and their *function* (how we *use* them in sentences):
   i. *Carrying* a heavy load is difficult.
   ii. *Carrying* a heavy load, he fell down.

In sentence i. *carrying* is used as a *noun*. Words that look like verbs but function as nouns (subjects and objects) are called *gerunds* or "verbal nouns." In sentence ii. *carrying* is used as a *modifier*. Like and *adjective*, *carrying* modifies *he*. (Notice the comma before *he*; the comma helps you to separate the modifying phrase from the subject of the sentence.)

2. "The Donkey in the Lion's Skin" uses verb + *ing* many times. Decide which ways verb + ing is used in these sentences from the fable. Mark each sentence G for gerund or M for modifier.
   a. Seeing him . . . , they thought him truly a Lion.
   b. Waving their front legs . . . , the oxen and horses reared up in the air.
   c. Shrieking, barking, bellowing, squealing, they ran up the dusty road.
   d. Carrying loads was the Donkey's proper business.

Exercise E: Questions for Discussion and Writing

1. Aesop doesn't tell us where this fable takes place. From the actions and descriptions in the fable, where do you think this story happened? What makes you think so?
2. Why would a Donkey want to look like a Lion?
3. If the Donkey were a human being in today's society, how would he think and feel about himself?
4. What kind of human being in today's society would this donkey-person want to be?
5. How would a donkey-person try to change himself into a lion-person? Would he be successful or not? If not, what mistakes would he make?
6. Close your book and think about this story. Then write about what happened to the donkey after he brayed instead of roaring like a lion. What did the people do to him? Use some words you learned from the story.

LESSON 2

The Milkmaid and Her Pail

SHARING EXPERIENCES

Compare your responses with those of your classmates.

- ❏ How are most farm products taken to market these days? How does this differ from the way food was transported long ago?
- ❏ Do you know of places today where people carry containers on their heads? If so, where? What is usually in the containers?
- ❏ What is the meaning of the expression "Do not count your chickens before they are hatched"? Does your language have a similar expression?
- ❏ Have you ever expected something to happen which did not occur? Did something unexpected happen instead? Describe the situation.

The Milkmaid and Her Pail

Adapted from Aesop

P atty, the milkmaid, was going to market, carrying her milk in a shiny *pail* on her head. As she went along, she began telling herself what she would do with all the money she would get for the milk.

2   "I'll buy some eggs from Farmer Brown," said she, "and put them under the little brown hen. Then the little brown hen will hatch me a lot of little chicks! And the little chicks will

---

pail — bucket; a container with a handle used for carrying milk or water.

grow up to be hens, and those hens will lay me dozens of eggs. I'll sell all the eggs for a great deal of money! Then with the money I get from the eggs, I'll buy a new white dress and a hat with pink flowers and blue ribbons. Oh, won't I look fine when I go to market in my new white dress and my hat with pink flowers and blue ribbons? Won't all my friends stand about and look at me? Polly Shaw will be there to stand and look, and Molly Parsons will be there to stand and look, and Jack Squires will be there to stand and look. But I shall just walk past them all and hold my chin high and toss my head like this —" As she spoke, she tossed her head back, the pail fell off and all the milk was spilled! So she had nothing at all to sell and all her fine dream was brought to nothing. She had to go home and tell her Mother what had happened.

3   "Ah, my child," said the Mother, "do not count your chickens before they are *hatched*."

---

hatched — out of their shells; born

EXERCISES

Exercise A: Recalling the Reading

Read each statement below and decide whether it is *true* or *false*. If the statement is false, correct it to make a true statement.

1. The milkmaid's name was Polly Parsons.
2. She was riding home on her bicycle.
3. The milkmaid was carrying chickens on her head.
4. She was planning to sell some eggs and make a lot of money.
5. Her mother owned a restaurant in town.
6. The milkmaid wanted a new dress and a new hat.
7. Jack Squires stole the milkmaid's pail of milk.
8. The milkmaid's mother said, "Don't cry over spilled milk."

Exercise B: Understanding the Reading

Summarize the main idea.

1. Quickly read the entire story again. In one sentence, tell your classmates what happened to the milkmaid.

2. Identify the person(s) or thing(s) referred to in each phrase. Pay special attention to the words in **boldface**.
   a. ". . . will grow up to be hens, . . ."
   b. "Oh, won't **I** look fine . . ."
   c. ". . . will be there to stand and look at me"
   d. ". . . **her** fine dream was brought to nothing"
   e. ". . . hold **my** chin high and toss **my** head like this —"

3. "Patty had to go home and tell her mother what happened." Imagine what they say to each other and write their words in the spaces.

   Mother: Well, Patty, you're home early.
   Patty: _____
   Mother: Where is your pail?
   Patty: _____

Mother: What happened to the milk?
Patty: _____
Mother: What were you doing?
Patty: _____
         _____

Mother: I see. Well, you know the old saying.
Patty: Which old saying?
Mother: _____

Exercise C: Analyzing Ideas

Choose the correct statement to complete the sentences below. You may have more than one answer for some sentences.

1. Patty was carrying milk to market because
   a. she was a milkmaid.
   b. she wanted to make some money.
   c. her mother was sick and poor.

2. Patty was going to sell the milk
   a. to buy eggs.
   b. to hatch chicks.
   c. to get some medicine for her mother.
   d. to buy a hat.

3. Patty was planning to buy a new dress and hat
   a. to look fine.
   b. to go to market.
   c. to impress her friends.

4. Patty's plans came to nothing because
   a. she stumbled and the pail fell off.
   b. she tossed her head and the pail fell off.
   c. the milk got sour.
   d. the pail had a hole in it.

5. Another way of telling the moral of this fable is:
   a. "Don't put all your eggs in one basket."
   b. "Don't cry over spilled milk."
   c. "A bird in the hand is worth two in the bush."

Exercise D: Word Study: Part One

All and its uses

1. i. The word *all* is used seven times in this fable. Find five examples like *"all* the money" (paragraph 1, line 3). Write down the examples.

   ii. In paragraph 2, lines 13 and 14, we find "But I shall just walk past *them all. . . ."* Is this usage like *"all* the money" or is it different? Can we say *"all of them"*?

   iii. Can we say "The money *all"* instead of *"all* the money"?

   iv. Which phrase do you use more often? *"all* (of). . . ." or ". . . *all"*?

2. In paragraph 2, line 16, we find "So she had nothing a*t all* to sell. . . ." Do you think that this usage is the same as the other five (see 1i) or is it different?

3. Use *all* (of) and *at all* in these sentences:
   a. He lost his money.
   b. I like your friends; I like them very much.
   c. She had nothing to say.
   d. John got the answers correct.
   e. Bill didn't understand the question.

Exercise D: Word Study: Part Two

Will and *won't*

   Patty, the milkmaid, uses *will* *('ll)* *(shall)* very often as she plans her future.

   i.   How many times do you find *will* or *'ll* or *shall*?

   ii. When *will* adds *not* to make a negative, the new word is *won't*: I *will* go — I *won't* go. For example, Patty says (paragraph 2, lines 10-12), "Oh, *won't* I look fine . . . ? *Won't* all my friends stand about . . . ?"

   iii. What does Patty mean?
       "I *won't* look fine. . . ."
       "All my friends *won't* stand about. . . ."
              or
       "I *will* look fine. . . ."
       "All my friends *will* stand about . . ."?

iv. What makes the difference in meaning?

v. When someone asks you, "Won't you come in?' "Won't you sit down?" "Won't you have more wine?" does the question mean, "You will not come in" / "you will not sit down" / "You will not have more wine," or does it mean the opposite?

Exercise E: Questions for Discussion and Writing

1. When do you think this story happened? What makes you think so?

2. Where do you think Patty lived? What makes you think so?

3. Does Patty have a problem? If you think so, how would you describe her problem?

4. What should Patty learn from her experience?

5. What do you think Patty will do *next* time on her way to market? Why do you think so?

6. Close your book and think about this story. Then write about what happened. Complete the following sentences:

The milkmaid was going to _____ , carrying

_____ . As she went along, she began telling

herself _____ . She planned to buy some eggs and

hatch them into _____ that would grow up into

_____ . She was going to sell _____ for

_____ . With the money she was going to

_____ . She wanted everybody to _____ .

As she was thinking about _____ , she held her

chin high and tossed _____ . When she did this,

the pail fell off and the milk _____ . So she had

_____ . Her mother told her _____ .

LESSON 3

The Bonfire and the Ants

The Writer and the Reading

ALEXANDER SOLZHENITSYN (1918 -   )

Alexander Solzhenitsyn now lives in the United States. He is a Russian writer whose most famous novels (*The First Circle*, *Cancer Ward* and *The Gulog Archipelago*) earned him the Nobel Prize in 1970. His novels were not published in the former Soviet Union because his work was critical of the government. Solzhenitsyn spent eight years in Soviet labor camps because of a "political crime"; consequently, much of his writing is autobiographical. Solzhenitsyn's themes are the betrayal of revolutionary ideals and the victory of the human spirit over suffering and misery.

   "The Bonfire and the Ants" is a very brief political fable or parable. Much of its power is the result of saying a great deal in a few lines.

Cultural Notes

When Alexander Solzhenitsyn came to live in the United States, he has been telling the world that the USSR — the Union of Soviet Socialist Republics (or the Soviet Union) — would cease to exist one day, and its people would be free. In 1991, his hope came true. Today there are several independent republics, but there is no longer a Soviet Union. Russia is the largest republic, and its leader at this time is Boris Yeltsin. We don't know what will happen to the republics or to the countries in Eastern Europe once controlled by the Soviet Union.

SHARING EXPERIENCES

Compare your responses with those of your classmates.

❏ Where have you seen ants? How did the ants behave? What do you know about the organization of ant colonies?

❏ Are there any similarities between ant colonies and human colonies?

❏ Here are some English words for sounds that a fire makes: *hiss, pop, crackle, whoosh*. Find one of these words in the story. Try to make these sounds.

❏ Have you seen ants around a fire? What did they do? What do people do when fire breaks out?

The Bonfire and the Ants

Alexander Solzhenitsyn

I threw a rotten log onto the fire without noticing that it was *alive with* ants.

2   The log began to crackle, the ants came *tumbling out* and *scurried around in desperation*. They ran along the top and *writhed* as they were scorched by the flames. I gripped the log and rolled it to one side. Many of the ants then *managed* to escape onto the sand or the *pine needles*.

3   But, strangely enough, they did not run away from the fire.

4   They had no sooner overcome their terror than they turned, circled and some kind of force drew them back to their *forsaken* homeland. There were many who climbed back onto the burning log, ran about on it, and *perished* there.

---

alive with — there were many ants on the log
tumbling out — falling out
scurried around in desperation — ran in total fear in all directions
writhed — rolled around in pain
managed to — were able to
pine needles — thin, long, pointed leaves of the pine tree
forsaken — lost; left
perished — died

EXERCISES

Exercise A: Recalling the Reading

Read each statement below and decide whether it is *true* or *false*. If the statement is false, correct it to make a true statement.

1. The log thrown on the fire was freshly cut.
2. The author saw the ants on the log before he threw it on the fire.
3. The ants tried to escape the fire.
4. The author helped the ants escape.
5. Most of the ants ran across the sand away from the fire.
6. A few ants returned to the burning log and perished.
7. The author compares the burning log to a forsaken homeland.

Exercise B: Understanding the Reading

Summarize the main idea.

1. Quickly read the entire story again. In one sentence, tell your classmates what happened.

2. Identify the person(s) or thing(s) referred to in each phrase. Pay special attention to the words in **boldface**.
   a. "Without noticing . . ."
   b. "**I** gripped the log and rolled it to one side."
   c. "scurried around in desperation. **They** . . . writhed as **they** were scorched by the flames."
   d. "**their** forsaken homeland."

Exercise C: Analyzing Ideas

Choose the correct statements to complete the sentences below.

1. The author of "The Bonfire and the Ants" rolled the log
   a. to make it burn more efficiently.
   b. to help the ants escape.
   c. to see the ants more easily.

2. The author expected the ants
   a. to return to their log.
   b. to run away from the fire.
   c. to stay near the fire.

3. The ants were drawn back to the fire
   a. by its light.
   b. by the warmth.
   c. by a force.

4. The author compares the burning log
   a. to a strong force.
   b. to a battle field.
   c. to a forsaken homeland.

5. Put the following statements in logical order to describe the action in the story.
   a. The ants ran about on the log and were burned.
   b. Some of the ants managed to escape onto the sand.
   c. Some of the ants circled and returned to the log.

6. The author implies that the ants are
   a. like refugees from a country.
   b. like animals who have been let out of a cage.
   c. like no other creatures.

7. The author is most interested in the _____ of the ants.
   a. description
   b. behavior
   c. environment

Exercise D: Word Study: Synonyms

Find the words in the reading that are similar in meaning to the word(s) in italics in each sentence. The number in parentheses at the end of each sentence tells you which paragraph in the reading contains the word you need.

1. I didn't *observe* that there were ants on the log. (1)
2. The ants *ran around* in all directions looking for an escape route. (2)
3. The firemen *were able* to rescue the child from the burning house. (2)
4. Ten people *died* when the train collided with the truck. (4)
5. He has *left* his wife and family and has disappeared. (4)
6. He *held tightly* to the life preserver until someone pulled him from the water. (2)
7. She finally *conquered* her fear of automobiles and learned to drive. (4)

Exercise E: Structure and Style

1. Match the nouns in Column A with the movement or sound they make in Column B. (For some items there may be more than one possible answer.)

Column A	Column B
1. brakes	a. wiggle
2. hands	b. grip
3. fire flames	c. clang
4. mice	d. crackle
5. snakes	e. scorch
6. bells	f. rattle
7. people in pain	g. tumble
8. airplanes	h. circle
9. babies	i. bang
10. firecrackers	j. scurry
11. small things in a box	k. screech
	l. writhe

2. Demonstrate as many of the movements or sounds above as you can.

3. Most human languages use words to imitate the sounds of nature. We call such words *echoic* (onomatopoeiac) because they *echo* the original sound. In English, bees *buzz*, snakes *hiss*, and *bow-wow* is the sound dogs make when they bark. Can you think of other words like these in English?

4. List some *echoic* words in other languages you know. Take turns pronouncing the words for your classmates and have them guess the meaning in English.

5. Make up words together for those sounds: a waterfall, leaves blowing in the wind, birds singing, glass breaking, hands rubbing together, a scratching sound on a blackboard.

Exercise F: Questions For Discussion and Writing

1. Whom do the ants in this story represent? What do the log, the man, and the fire represent?

2. What are some reasons that people might want to leave their country?

3. Name some countries which people have recently left in large numbers. Why did they leave?

4. Do refugees often try to return to their home countries? Why or why not?

5. Is this story about the refugees' love of their homeland? Explain your answer.

6. After you have read "The Bonfire and the Ants," think about paragraph 4. Will some of the newly freed Soviet citizens choose to return to the old ways?

7. Close your book and think about this story. Why did the ants go back to the fire? What happened to them? Does the phrase "their forsaken homeland" apply only to the ants? Whom else might the phrase apply to? Use some words you learned from the story.

LESSON 4

The Unicorn in the Garden

The Writer and the Reading

JAMES THURBER (1894 – 1961)

James Thurber made his reputation as a very witty critic of life through hundreds of cartoons and collections of short stories and fables. Few people looking at his drawings or reading his stories would guess that Thurber was nearly blind for much of his adult life. Drawing and writing were painful and difficult for him. How remarkable, then, that he produced so much pleasure for others.

Thurber plays with the conflict between men and women in an amusing way, but underneath the humorous surface there is a seriousness of purpose. "The Unicorn in The Garden" is a modern fable. It is more than a funny story.

SHARING EXPERIENCES

Compare your responses with those of your classmates. Look at the picture of a unicorn.

❏ What real animal does the unicorn look like?
  • Do you have a name for this mythical (unreal) creature in your language?
  • Are there stories about unicorns in your language?
  • What magical powers does a unicorn have?
  • What other mythical creatures appear in stories in your language?

❏ Think about the way American husbands and wives relate to each other. Then compare their relationship with the husband-wife relationships in your culture.

❏ Are there common jokes or funny stories about husbands and wives in your culture? If so, share one with your classmates.

❏ Have you ever seen a straitjacket? What is it? What is its purpose?

❏ What happens to people who are mentally ill in your country? Where do they go? What kind of medical care do they receive?

The Unicorn in the Garden

James Thurber

Once upon a sunny morning a man who sat in a *breakfast nook* looked up from his scrambled eggs to see a white unicorn with a golden horn quietly eating the roses in the garden. The man went up to the bedroom where his wife was still asleep and woke her up. "There's a *unicorn* in the garden," he said.

---

breakfast nook — a small area in or near the kitchen where informal meals are eaten
unicorn — an animal with a single horn on its head

"Eating roses." She opened up one unfriendly eye and looked at him, "The unicorn is a *mythical beast*" she said, and turned her back on him. The man walked slowly downstairs and out into the garden. The unicorn was still there; he was now *munching* some of the tulips. "Here, unicorn," said the man, and he pulled up a lily and gave it to him. The unicorn ate it *gravely*.

2   *With a high heart* because there was a unicorn in his garden, the man went upstairs and woke up his wife again. "The unicorn," he said, "ate a *lily*. I pulled it up myself." His wife sat herself up in bed and looked at him coldly. "You are a *booby*," she said, "and I am going to have you put in the *booby-hatch*." The man, who had never liked the words "booby" and "booby-hatch" and who liked them even less on a shining morning when there was a unicorn in the garden, thought it over for a moment. "We'll see about that," he said. He walked over to the door. "He has a golden horn in the middle of his forehead," he told her. Then he went back to the garden to watch the unicorn; but the unicorn had gone away. The man sat down among the roses and went to sleep.

3   As soon as the husband had gone out of the house, the wife got up and put on her clothes as fast as she could. She was very excited and there was *a gloat in her eye*. She telephoned the police and she telephoned a *psychiatrist*; she told them to hurry and bring a *straitjacket*. When the police and the psychiatrist arrived they sat down in chairs and looked at her with great interest. "My husband," she said, "saw a unicorn this morn-

---

mythical beast — an imaginary animal
munching — eating slowly
gravely — seriously
with a high heart — he was very happy
booby — a crazy person (slang expression)
booby hatch — a hospital where crazy people live (slang expression)
a gloat in her eye — she was feeling mean and nasty
psychiatrist — a doctor for people with mental and emotional problems
straitjacket — a jacket with long sleeves that can be tied around a person if he/she is wild and hard to control

ing." The police looked over at the psychiatrist and the psychiatrist looked over at the police. "He told me it ate a lily," she said. The psychiatrist looked over at the police and the police looked over at the psychiatrist. "He told me it had a golden horn in the middle of its forehead," she said. At a *solemn signal* from the psychiatrist, the police leaped from their chairs and seized the wife. They had a hard time subduing her, for she put up *a terrific struggle*, but they finally subdued her. Just as they got her into the straitjacket, the husband came back into the house.

4. "Did you tell your wife you saw a unicorn?" asked the police. "Of course not," said the husband. "The unicorn is a mythical beast." "That's all I wanted to know," said the psychiatrist. "Take her away. I'm sorry, sir, but your wife is *as crazy as a jaybird*." So they took her away, *cursing and screaming*, and shut her up in an *institution*. The husband lived happily ever after.

Moral: Don't count your boobies until they are hatched.

---

solemn signal — a serious gesture of the hand
a terrific struggle — a hard fight
as crazy as a jaybird — (slang) mentally ill
cursing and screaming — yelling bad words and shouting
institution — mental hospital

EXERCISES

Exercise A: Recalling the Reading

Read each statement below and tell whether it is *true* or *false*. If the statement is false, correct it to make a true statement.

1. This story began in the morning.
2. The unicorn had a silver horn.
3. The man's wife saw the unicorn.
4. The wife said, "The unicorn is a mythical beast."
5. The man talked to the unicorn.
6. The wife telephoned a psychiatrist.
7. The police and the psychiatrist thought the woman was crazy.
8. She went quietly to an institution.

Exercise B: Understanding the Reading

Summarize the main idea.

1. Quickly read the entire story again. Tell your classmates what finally happened to the wife.

2. Identify the person(s) or thing(s) referred to in each phrase. Pay special attention to the words in **boldface**.
   a. "... sat in a breakfast nook ..."
   b. "**She** opened up one unfriendly eye and looked at him ..."
   c. "**He** was now munching on some tulips."
   d. "**I** am going to have to put you in the booby hatch."
   e. "... sat down among the roses and went to sleep."
   f. "... there was a gloat in **her** eye."
   g. "... **they** ... looked at her with great interest."
   h. "... looked over at the psychiatrist ..."
   i. "**They** had a hard time subduing her ..."
   j. "... crazy as a jaybird."

Exercise C: Analyzing Ideas

Choose the correct statements to complete the sentences below. You may have more than one answer for some sentences.

1. The man
   a. enjoyed seeing the unicorn.
   b. pretended that he saw a unicorn.
   c. didn't like unicorns.

2. The man's wife didn't go down to the garden because
   a. she didn't believe her husband's story about the unicorn.
   b. she didn't like her husband.
   c. she was afraid of the unicorn.

3. The wife called her husband a booby because
   a. she thought he was crazy.
   b. she thought he was very smart.
   c. she wanted him to go to a booby hatch.

4. The husband said, "We'll see about that" because
   a. he wanted to go to the booby hatch.
   b. he knew that the unicorn was real.
   c. he knew that the police wouldn't believe his wife's story.

5. The woman told the police and psychiatrist to bring a straitjacket because
   a. her husband was asleep in the garden.
   b. she expected her husband to struggle when they tried to take him away.
   c. she needed one.

6. The police took the woman away in the straitjacket because
   a. her husband struggled terrifically.
   b. she asked them to bring it.
   c. they thought that she was crazy.

7. The man lived happily ever after because
   a. he had seen a unicorn.
   b. his wife was gone.
   c. he liked being in a booby hatch.

Exercise D: Word Study: Making Connections

The words in the left-hand list are related to words in the right-hand list. What combinations can you make? Try to form grammatical sentences using the combinations. You may change the order of the words.

happily	husband
booby	wife
crazy	unicorn
mythical	garden
unfriendly	psychiatrist
roses	police
lily	
munching	
white	
coldly	
straitjacket	
gloat	
subdued	
screaming	
tulips	

Exercise E: Structure and Style

In "The Unicorn in the Garden," James Thurber often uses a basic sentence structure: sentence 1 *and* sentence 2.

> *Example*:

> "{The man went up to the bedroom where his wife was still asleep} {and woke her up.}" (Paragraph 1)

Two completed actions — *went up* and *woke* — are combined in one sentence.

1. In "The Unicorn in the Garden" James Thurber joins words and sentences with *and*. Other examples of using *and* to join sentences are these:

    (1) Here, unicorn," said the man, *and* pulled up a lily *and* gave it to him. (Three sentences combined into one sentence.)

(2) She telephoned the police *and* she telephoned a psychiatrist. . . . (Two sentences combined into one sentence.)

This little word *and* is very important. It shows us a relationship between the contents of the sentences that are joined together to make a new sentence.

2. Underline or write down all of the examples of sentence combining you can find in Thurber's story.

3. Now remove all the *ands* between sentences. Use a period to punctuate complete sentences. Add nouns or pronouns when it is necessary.

   Example: "The man sat down among the roses and went to sleep."

   The man sat down among the roses.

   (The man/He) went to sleep.

4. How does the style of the story change when you change compound sentences to single sentences? Does the story move more easily or less easily after you remove the *ands*?

Exercise F: Questions for Discussion and Writing

1. Do you think the wife and husband in the story love each other and enjoy each other's company? Give information from the story to support your answer.

2. Do you think the husband is crazy? Why or why not?

3. Are you familiar with the expression "Don't count your chickens before they are hatched"? How does this moral apply to Thurber's story?

4. Thurber's humor is often based on "playing with words." How is the moral of "The Unicorn in the Garden" an example of this? (Compare it to the English proverb quoted in The Milkmaid and Her Pail (pages 11-12)

5. After you finish reading "The Unicorn in the Garden," come back to this picture and try to answer this question: What is

the relationship between this drawing (page 24) and the
fable? Both the drawing and the fable are by James Thurber.

6. Here is a simple summary of the story you have just read
and studied. Fill in the blanks with words that make sense
and are grammatically correct. You can go back to the
story and use words from it, or you can use words that you
already know.

One _____ a man was _____ breakfast.
He _____ a _____ eating _____ in the
garden. The man _____ his wife about the
_____ . She told him that he was _____ .
She said, "You are a _____ ."

The wife _____ the _____ and she
_____ a psychiatrist. She _____ them to
bring a _____ .

When they _____ , the wife _____ them
that her husband _____ a _____ that
morning. "The _____ _____ a lily," she said.
The police _____ the wife and put her in a
_____ .

The police asked the husband, "Did you _____
your _____ you _____ a _____ ?"
The husband said, " _____ course _____ .
The _____ is a _____ beast."

The _____ and the _____ took the wife
_____ , and the _____ lived _____
_____ after.

2

Sorrows

LESSON 5

A White Man's Word

The Writer

DEBRA SWALLOW (1954 –   )

Debra Swallow is a Native American (Oglala) writer. She says this about herself: "I was born in 1954. Went to school at Oglala Community College. I live in Manderson, South Dakota." Her work has appeared in several collections of writing by women.

The Reading

There's an old saying in American society: "Sticks and stones may break my bones, but names will never hurt me." Names aren't *things* like sticks and stones. Calling people bad names can't hurt because there is no physical damage, like a cut or a bruise.

However, when you think of all the injuries and deaths caused by *words*, you know that the old saying often isn't true. We *wish* that names didn't hurt, but often they do, especially names like "Nigger" (for African American), "Chink" (for Chinese), and the name used in Debra Swallow's story, "half-breed" (someone having one white and one non-white parent). Name-calling is part of *racism*, a conflict between the majority — white Americans — and the minorities — Americans of different colors and beliefs. Racism has a long and miserable history in American culture and in the cultures of many other nations. In recent years there have been positive developments in interracial relationships in America, but racism continues.

In Debra Swallow's story, the term "Indian" is used by the narrator. Many people prefer the term "Native American." The term "Lakota" refers to a Native American tribe.

SHARING EXPERIENCES

Compare your responses with those of your classmates.

❏ These are the names of some Native American (Indian) tribes: Apache, Lakota, Comanche, Chippewa, Yakima, Tulalip, Iroquois, Sioux, Navajo, Hopi. Can you name others? Find out where they used to live in the United States. Where are their reservations now? What else do you know about them?

❏ Are you of mixed racial or cultural background? What is your cultural heritage? Does your culture have a name for people who are of mixed race? Is it a positive or negative term?

❏ Have you ever had someone talk badly to you about your heritage? What did you say or do? How did you feel?

❏ When you were a child, did you go swimming in the summer? Where did you like to swim? Did you eat popsicles? What other treats did you eat?

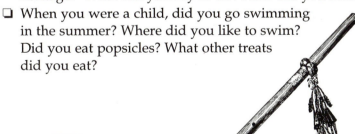

A White Man's Word

Debra Swallow

The screen door slammed shut, and I just knew eighty flies came in. Then I heard *wailing and gibberish* and ran to see who it was. My nine-year-old son was running toward me with blood, tears and dirty sweat *trickling off* his chin, making my knees go weak.

2   "What happened? Who did this to you?" I asked, kneeling to wipe his round face with a cool, damp cloth.

---

wailing and gibberish — crying and unclear talking
trickling off — running down

3   "I got in a fight, Mom. Mom, what's a half-breed?"

4   I felt like my blood stopped running, and I closed my eyes to kill my tears, my mind opening up to a day I'd almost forgotten.

❏ ❏ ❏

5   I opened my eyes to see how underwater looked, and a sting like *cactus tips* closed them fast. Surfacing, I looked across the pool for my friend. The water shimmered turquoise blue, reflecting nothing but the painted concrete bottom and rectangles of green light from the roof. Forty or fifty pale faces and arms *bobbed* and floated above the water, but no sign of my friend's brown, familiar face.

6   "Maybe it's time to go," I thought and swam to the closest edge. Feeling rough, *slimy* cement on the palms of my hands, I hauled myself out of the water. Unsure of my footing, I walked slowly toward the shower rooms.

7   Screams, *giggles* and little-girl conversation filled the room, along with spraying, splashing and draining water. Stooping to *peek* under the first shower stall, I saw two white feet and moved on to the second door. Also two white feet. Next door, four white feet. I could feel myself starting to shiver now and my breath felt trapped in my chest. "What if they left me? I don't know anybody here," I thought.

8   My friend and her mom took me with them to Rushville to swim. My first time alone away from my family, and here I was, scared among white people — the only Indian in sight.

9   I decided to *just kind of stand around* in the shower room. I knew she wasn't in the pool, so she had to come here, where our clothes were. Trying to be as unnoticeable as possible, I leaned against a cool, wet wall and watched the white girls in the room, curious because I'd never been around any before.

---

cactus tips — thorns; parts of a plant that cause pain
bobbed — moved up and down
slimy — slippery
giggles — silly laughter
peek — look quickly; glance
just kind of stand around — wait

10   "My dad bought me a brand-new bike and it has a blue daisy basket on the handlebars," one girl *whined* to her friend. "Well, I already knew that, but did you know my dad bought me a new bed and it has a *canopy* on it?" she whined back in a sing-song voice. The two girls were probably eight years old like me, but both were *chubby* with blonde *ringlets* and painted toenails.

11   Spacing out their words, I was thinking about the bike Dad made my sister and me. He made it from all different parts he found at the *trash pile*, and it looked funny and rusty, but it worked real well. Daddy also made us a pair of *stilts*, a play-house and a *pogo stick*, which all our friends wanted to play with. I knew my dad was better than theirs; he BUILT stuff for us.

12   I noticed the first girl was dressed now, and while waiting for her friend to finish, she pulled out a whole handful of red *licorice* and chewed on one while her friend *jabbered*, every once in a while glancing at me, not knowing my tongue ached to taste just one mouthful of her licorice. Every time she looked at me, I wanted to *evaporate*. I had on a borrowed swimsuit a size too big, dull and old-fashioned compared to the bright-colored flower- or print-covered two-pieces all the other girls wore. My hair hung down my back, straight and dark and thick.

13   The first girl said, "Look, this Indian is staring at us," and glared at me with icy blue eyes, her nose pointing to the ceiling. The second girl said. "Oh, she don't know what we're saying

---

whined — spoke in a high-pitched voice
canopy — overhead cover
chubby — overweight; plump
ringlets — small rings of hair
trash pile — dump; a place for discarded things
stilts — tall sticks that children stand and walk on, making themselves taller
pogo stick — a stick with a spring for jumping
licorice — a kind of candy made in long strings
jabbered — talked rapidly and loudly
evaporate — here, disappear

anyhow. Dirty Indians don't know anything." Her friend said, "I don't think she's really a real Indian. My dad says some of them are half-breeds. So she's not **all** dirty."

14 "Only half-dirty," her friend said, and they giggled together and laughed at me.

15 My face felt hot and my arms were heavy as I walked carefully across the wet, slippery floor towards them. I noticed from far away that the room's noises started to *fade*.

16 I grabbed one of them by her hair and threw her away, wrapped my arm around the other one's neck and wrestled her down, and sitting on her, I kept punching her till her friend grabbed me. I stood up, and jerking away, I tripped her, landing her by her friend. They were both still crying and screaming on the floor when I walked out, carrying my bundle of clothes under my arm.

17 Standing outside in the shade of the pool building, I was really scared. There was someone yelling, "Debi! Debi!" but I wouldn't look. Somehow I thought they found out my name and were going to do something to me. But it was my friend's mom; she and my friend went for *popsicles* and just got back. I ran to their car and told them what I did, so my friend's mom went in after the clothes my friend left in the shower room and we headed back for home.

18 Safe once again with my family, I told Mom and Dad I got in a fight.

19 "Daddy, what's a half-breed?" I asked him.

20 The house got quiet; the only sound was the wind. Daddy looked at me and his eyes were sad.

21 "My girl, you're an Indian. The way of living is Indian. Lakota."

22 I said, "Yes, but what is a half-breed?"

23 "A white man's word," is what he said. "It's just a white man's word."

---

fade — become less
popsicles — frozen fruit juice on a stick

❏ ❏ ❏

24 Now, eighteen years later, I was wiping blood from my son's face, and his question made my body shake with anger, sadness, frustration and hatred. Opening my eyes, I answered, "You're Lakota, son. The way of living is Indian. You're Lakota." He looked at me with black eyes shining with tears he now *refused to shed*, and asked me again what a half-breed was.

25 "A white man's word," is what I said. "It's just a white man's word."

---

refused to shed — could not release

EXERCISES

Exercise A: Recalling the Reading

Read each statement below and tell whether it is *true* or *false*. If the statement is false, correct it to make a true statement.

1. The narrator refers to herself as an Indian.
2. The narrator refers to herself as a half-breed.
3. The narrator is 14 years old.
4. The narrator is scared of white people.
5. The narrator comes from a large middle-class family.
6. The narrator is curious about white people.
7. The narrator beat up the white girls because she enjoyed fighting.
8. Lakota is one of the states in the United States.

Exercise B: Understanding the Reading

Summarize the main idea.

1. Quickly read the entire story again. In one sentence tell your classmates why the narrator grabbed and punched the two girls in the shower room.

2. Identify the person(s) or thing(s) referred to in each phrase. Pay special attention to the words in **boldface**.
   a. "... was running toward me with blood, tears and dirty sweat trickling off **his** chin, making my knees go weak."
   b. "Forty or fifty pale faces and arms bobbed and floated above the water ..."
   c. " 'What if they left me? I don't know anybody here,' **I** thought."
   d. "Well, **I** already knew that, but did you know **my** dad bought **me** a new bed and it has a canopy on it?"
   e. "... also made us a pair of stilts, a playhouse and a pogo stick, which all our friends wanted to play with."
   f. "Dirty **Indians** don't know anything."

g. "... she and my friend went for popsicles and just got back."

h. "The way of living is Indian. Lakota."

Exercise C: Analyzing Ideas

Choose correct statements to complete the sentences below.

1. The story opens with the narrator
    a. having a fight.
    b. stopping a fight.
    c. questioning her nine-year-old son.

2. The narrator once had
    a. a fight with white girls.
    b. a white girl as her best friend.
    c. a white husband.

3. The narrator is
    a. ashamed of her family.
    b. proud of her family.
    c. tired of her family.

4. The swimming party at Rushville is
    a. a weekly event.
    b. a family outing.
    c. the narrator's first time away from her family.

5. The narrator beats up the two white girls because
    a. they giggled.
    b. they had new bicycles.
    c. they insulted her.

6. The narrator remembers her fight because
    a. her son got in a fight.
    b. her son was called a half-breed.
    c. her father told her what a half-breed was.
    d. all of the above.

Exercise D: Word Study: Antonyms

Debra Swallow's story depends on *opposites* to make the conflict real. To see how the opposition works, look at the examples from the story. Then try to find words that mean the opposite and write them in the space provided.

forty or fifty *pale* faces	brown faces
brown, familiar face	pale face
two *white* feet	_____
unsure of my footing	_____
scared among white people	_____
as *unnoticeable* as possible	_____
I wanted to *evaporate*	_____
a *dull* and *old-fashioned* swimsuit	_____
my hair . . . *straight* and *dark* and *thick*	_____
I walked *carefully*	_____
". . . You're an *Indian*. . . ."	_____

What happens to the character of the narrator when you substitute opposites?

Exercise E: Questions for Discussion and Writing

1. Why does the story open with a fight?
2. Why does the narrator "just kind of stand around" if she wants to be "unnoticeable"?
3. Why does the narrator remember the bicycle her Dad made from "trash"?
4. Why does the narrator beat up the two white girls?
5. Did the fight solve any problems? What did the fight accomplish?
6. What should the narrator have done when the white girl said "half-breed" and "half-dirty"?

7. What does "a white man's word" really mean? Does it answer the question "... but what is a half-breed?"

8. What advice should the narrator give her nine-year-old son about the topics below? List the statements you would say or write to a nine-year-old boy who has just been in a fight over "names."
   - color
   - racial or ethnic group
   - name-calling
   - fighting

9. Close your book and think about the story. Write the answer to this question: Why does the term "half-breed" make the Native Americans in this story feel sad?

LESSON 6

The Geese

The Writer

E. B. WHITE (1899-1985)

E. B. White had a very long and productive life as a writer. He began his writing career in 1921, when he was just out of college. His work as a newspaper reporter was not successful: "I was almost useless," White said.

His success as a writer began in 1925, when he joined *The New Yorker* magazine; this relationship continued for forty years.

Most critics praise White as an essayist — some say he is one of the best essayists of the twentieth century. He must also be acknowledged as one of the best writers of stories, especially stories for children. *Charlotte's Web* and *Stuart Little*, are classics in children's literature.

The Reading

In the middle of the Depression, in 1934, E. B. White and his wife, Katharine Angell, bought a farm in North Brooklin, Maine. White wanted to live close to the land in order to keep alive "the precious sense for basic things."

In 1938, White and his wife moved to the farm permanently and they began to raise geese, chickens, and sheep. Their experiences were collected in a monthly column, "One Man's Meat," that White wrote for *Harper's* magazine. "The Geese" comes from *The New Yorker*.

As you know from reading Aesop and Thurber, animal fables have been part of human culture for many centuries. Although "The Geese" is not really an animal fable, White's story or "familiar essay" uses the behavior of animals — geese, in this case — to show us a *larger* truth that applies to human beings, too. Geese are supposed to mate for life. So are people, if we can believe the marriage vows.

White's female geese have interesting names, Apathy and Liz. The first means a lack of feeling; the second is a common abbreviation for Elizabeth. The male geese — the ganders — are simply old and young; they have no names. The interaction of animal and human behavior is at the heart of "The Geese."

SHARING EXPERIENCES

Compare your responses with those of your classmates.

❑ Have you ever lived on a farm? Did the farm have chickens, geese, ducks or turkeys?

❑ English cookbooks group these birds (turkey, geese, ducks, chickens) under the terms *fowl* or *poultry*. How are these birds different from other birds such as robins or sparrows?

❑ Describe the difference between the behavior of the male and female fowl. Which birds sit on nests until the eggs hatch (males or females)?

❑ Below are some words to help you talk about domestic birds commonly found on farms. Add the English names for other fowl which are familiar to you.

	Male	**Female**	**Baby**
Geese	gander	goose	gosling
Chickens	rooster	hen	chick
Ducks	drake	duck	duckling
Turkeys	tom	hen	chick

❑ Have you ever seen fowl or other bird eggs hatch? Did all the eggs in the nest hatch? Why/why not? What kind of fowl or bird eggs were they?

❑ Have you ever witnessed male fowl, birds, or animals fighting with each other? Why were they fighting? How did you feel when you saw them?

The Geese

E. B. White

During the last week in May, Apathy, having produced only three eggs of her own but having *acquired* ten through the *kind offices* of her sister and me, became *broody* and began to sit. Liz, with a *tally* of twenty-five eggs, ten of them stolen, showed not the slightest desire to sit. Laying was *her thing*. She laid and laid, while the other goose sat and sat. The old gander, *marveling* at what he had *wrought*, showed a great deal of interest in both nests. The young gander was impressed but subdued. I continued to remove the early eggs from Liz's nest, holding her to a *clutch* of fifteen and *discarding* the extras. In late

---

acquired — got, gotten
kind offices — help
broody — ready to sit on a nest
tally — count   **her thing** — her preference
marveling — greatly surprised
wrought — done; made   **clutch** — group
discarding — throwing away

June, having produced forty-one eggs, ten of which were under Apathy, she at last sat down.

2   I had marked Apathy's hatching date on my desk calendar. On the night before the *goslings* were due to arrive, when I *made my rounds* before going to bed, I looked in on her. She hissed, as usual, and ran her neck out. When I shone my light at her, two tiny green heads were visible, thrusting their way through her feathers. The goslings were here — a few hours ahead of schedule. My heart leapt up. Outside, in the barnyard, both ganders *stood vigil*. They knew very well *what was up*: ganders take an enormous interest in family affairs and are deeply impressed by the miracle of the egg-that-becomes-goose. I shut the door against them and went to bed.

3   Next morning, Sunday, I rose early and went straight to the barn to see what the night had brought. Apathy was sitting quietly while five goslings *teetered* about on the slopes of the nest. One of them, as I watched, *strayed from* the others, and, not being able to find his way back, began sending out cries for help. They were the kind of *distress signal* any anxious father would instantly respond to. Suddenly, I heard sounds of a rumble outside in the barnyard where the ganders were — loud sounds of scuffling. I ran out. A fierce fight was in progress — it was no mere *skirmish*, it was the real thing. The young gander had grabbed the old one by the *stern*, his white head buried in feathers right where it would hurt the most, and was running him around the yard, *punishing* him at every turn — *thrusting* him on ahead and beating him unmercifully with his wings.

---

goslings — baby geese
made my rounds — made my visits
stood vigil — watched over the geese
what was up — what was happening
teetered — walked unsteadily
strayed from — left
distress signal — sound of trouble
skirmish — small battle
stern — rear end
punishing — hurting
thrusting — pushing

4 It was an *awesome* sight, these two great male birds locked in combat, *slugging it out* — not for the favors of a female but for the *dubious* privilege of assuming the responsibilities of parenthood. The young male had suffered all spring the *indignities* of a *restricted life* at the pond; now he had turned, at last, against the old one, as though to get even. Round and round, over rocks and through weeds, they raced, struggling and tripping, the old one *in full retreat* and in apparent pain. It was a beautiful late-June morning, with fair-weather clouds and a light wind going, the grasses long in the orchard — the kind of morning that always carries for me *overtones* of summer sadness, I don't know why. Overhead, three swallows circled at low altitude, pursuing one white feather, the *coveted trophy* of nesting time. They were like three tiny fighter planes giving air support to the battle that raged below. For a moment, I thought of climbing the fence and trying to separate the combatants, but instead I just watched. The engagement was soon over. Plunging desperately down the lane, the old gander sank to the ground. The young one let go, turned, and walked back, screaming in triumph, to the door behind which his newly won family were waiting: a strange family indeed — the sister who was not even the mother of the babies, and the babies who were not even his own *get*.

5 When I was sure the fight was over, I climbed the fence and closed the barnyard gate, effectively separating *victor from vanquished*. The old gander had risen to his feet. He was in almost the same spot in the lane where his first wife had died mysteriously more than a year ago. I watched as he *threaded his way* slowly down the narrow path between clumps of thistles

---

awesome — frightening
slugging it out — beating each other up
dubious — doubtful; unlikely
indignities — bad treatment
restricted life — limited activities
in full retreat — running away
overtones — suggestions; hints
coveted trophy — desired reward
get — "children"; goslings
victor from vanquished — winner from loser
threaded his way — walked carefully

and daisies. His head was barely visible above the grasses, but his broken spirit was plain to any eye. When he reached the *pasture bars*, he hesitated, then painfully *squatted* and eased himself under the bottom bar and into the pasture, where he sat down on the *cropped sward* in the bright sun. I felt very deeply his sorrow and his defeat. *As things go in the animal kingdom*, he is about my age, and when he lowered himself to creep under the bar, I could feel in my own bones his pain at bending down so far. Two hours later, he was still sitting there, the sun by this time quite hot. I had seen *his likes* often enough on the benches of the treeless main street of a Florida city — spent old males, motionless in the glare of the day.

6   Toward the end of the morning, he walked back up the lane as far as the gate, and there he stood all afternoon, his head and orange bill looking like the head of a great snake. The goose and her goslings had *emerged* into the barnyard. Through the space between the boards of the gate, the old fellow watched the *enchanting* scene: the goslings taking their frequent drinks of water, climbing in and out of the shallow pan for their first swim, closely guarded by the handsome young gander, *shepherded* by the pretty young goose.

7   After supper, I went into the *tie-ups* and pulled the five remaining, unhatched eggs from the nest and thought about the five lifeless chicks inside the eggs — the unlucky ones, the ones that lacked what it takes to break out of an egg into the light of a fine June morning. I put the eggs in a basket and set the basket with some other *miscellany consigned to the dump*. I don't know anything sadder than a summer's day.

---

pasture bars — fence between the field and the road
squatted — sat down
cropped sward — cut grass
as things go in the animal kingdom — as we count years
his likes — others like him
emerged — come out
enchanting — very pleasant
shepherded — looked after; guided
tie-ups — cages; roosts
miscellany — various things
consigned to the dump — items to be thrown into the garbage

EXERCISES

Exercise A: Recalling the Reading

Read each statement and decide whether it is *true* or *false*. If the statement is false, correct it to make a true statement.

1. "The Geese" takes place in the fall.
2. Apathy laid eggs, but Liz sat on them.
3. The young gander attacked the old gander.
4. The narrator of the story separated the two ganders.
5. The old gander was injured in the fight.
6. The narrator of the story disliked the young gander and locked him out of the yard.
7. The narrator and his wife ate the unhatched eggs.

Exercise B: Understanding the Reading

Summarize the main idea.

1. In one sentence, tell your classmates how the author felt about the old gander.
2. Identify the person(s) or thing(s) referred to in each phrase. Pay special attention to the words in **boldface**.
   a. "Laying was **her** thing."
   b. ". . . marveling at what **he** had wrought, showed a great deal of interest in both nests."
   c. "**She** hissed, as usual, and ran **her** neck out."
   d. "**My** heart leapt up."
   e. ." . . **his** white head buried in feathers right where it would hurt the most, and was running him around the yard, punishing him at every turn — thrusting him on ahead and beating him unmercifully with **his** wings."
   f. "**They** were like three tiny fighter planes giving air support to the battle that raged below."
   g. ". . . let go, turned, and walked back, screaming in triumph, to the door behind which **his** newly won family were waiting . . ."

h. "**His** head was barely visible above the grasses, but **his** broken spirit was plain to any eye."

i. "I had seen **his likes** often enough on the benches of the treeless main street of a Florida city — **spent old males**, motionless in the glare of day."

Exercise C: Analyzing Ideas

Choose correct statements to complete the sentences below.

1. The narrator removes eggs from Liz's nest
   a. to eat them.
   b. to give them to Apathy.
   c. to sell them to other farmers.

2. Both ganders stood vigil in the barnyard because
   a. both ganders are parents.
   b. both ganders are interested in nests and the birth of young geese.
   c. the two ganders are friends.

3. The young gander attacked the old gander
   a. to teach him a lesson.
   b. to become a parent.
   c. to impress the geese.

4. After the fight the old gander was
   a. seriously wounded and bleeding.
   b. not seriously wounded but broken in spirit.
   c. a good loser and as cheerful as ever.

5. The moral of "The Geese" is
   a. Don't count your goslings until they're hatched.
   b. A bird in the cage is worth two in the pasture.
   c. Don't put all your eggs in one basket.
   d. None of the above.

Exercise D: Word Study: Characters and Their Modifiers

E. B. White has presented us with a little drama, and its parts are played by two geese, Apathy and Liz; two ganders, old and young; several goslings; and the narrator, a middle-aged writer named E. B. White.

As you think about these characters, remember how they looked and how they acted. Adjectives and verbs — *-ing* forms and *-ed* forms — present the appearance and behavior of the characters. Which of these modifiers best describes one or more of the characters? In the space provided after the modifiers, write in the name(s) of the characters.

a. stood vigil   _____

b. beating, punishing, thrusting   _____

c. struggling and tripping   _____

d. slugging it out   _____

e. plunging   _____

f. screaming   _____

g. laying   _____

h. sitting   _____

i. marveling   _____

j. teetered   _____

k. discarding   _____

l. hissed   _____

m. painfully squatted   _____

n. shepherded   _____

o. climbing in and out   _____

p. felt very deeply   _____

q. just watched   _____

r. broken spirit   _____

s. heart leapt up   _____

t. tiny green heads   _____

Which characters receive most of the description? Why do you think this happens?

Exercise E: Questions for Discussion and Writing

1. Does the writer seem more sympathetic toward one of the characters in "The Geese"? How does he show his sympathy?
2. Why do you think the young gander attacks the old gander?
3. Why doesn't the narrator separate the battling ganders and stop the fight?
4. What does the young gander win? What is his prize?
5. When the narrator tells us (paragraph 4) "I had seen his likes often enough . . . ," what is the comparison he is trying to make?
6. Why do you think "The Geese" ends with the line "I don't know anything sadder than a summer's day"?
7. Close your book and think about this story. Then answer this question: Why did the narrator of the story feel so deeply about the old gander's sorrow and defeat?

Exercise F: Additional Activity

Think about "The Geese" and its characters, its conflicts, and its ending. Here are three sayings or proverbs:

> "Might makes right."
> "To the victor go the spoils."
> "All is fair in love and war."

Be sure that you understand what each proverb means: that is, how the key words "might," "right," "spoils," and "fair" are being used.

Then select *one* of the proverbs as a title for a passage you will write about "The Geese." Explain how the title fits the characters, the action, and the ending of "The Geese." If you think that *none* of the titles fits, you can write about that, too. If you can think of a better title of your own, use it and write about its relationship to "The Geese."

LESSON 7

Thank you, Ma'm

The Writer

LANGSTON HUGHES (1902–1967)

Langston Hughes is one of several "voices" for the African-American people in the U.S., along with James Weldon Johnson, Countee Cullen, Richard Wright, James Baldwin, Lorraine Hansberry, and a number of younger African American writers. Hughes may be the best African American poet to come out of the American experience. His later poetry expresses the anger and frustration of the African American people, and he warned the white people in America with these lines: "You're the one / yes, you're the one / will have the blues. . . ."

Hughes wrote a good deal of prose, too, and his story "Thank You Ma'm" has its roots in the African American culture and the sense of human decency which Hughes knew well and believed in. He chose to live in Harlem even after he became a famous writer.

The Reading

The language that the writer uses in this story is the kind of speech we often hear in the street. The grammar is different from that of standard English. Mrs. Jones says, "Now ain't you ashamed of yourself?" and ". . . I would not take you nowhere" and "Ain't you got nobody home . . ." There are other examples of the use of *ain't* for *aren't* or *haven't* and other examples of the "double negative": would *not* . . . *no*where.

In addition to changes in grammar, Mrs. Jones uses

expressions like "I got a great mind to . . ." and "You got another thought coming" and ". . . latching onto my pocketbook. . . ." These are changes in *word* usage, common expressions we sometimes call "idioms" or "informal dialect."

Why do you think Langston Hughes's characters, Mrs. Jones and Roger, talk this way?

SHARING EXPERIENCES

Compare your responses with those of your classmates.

❑ How do streets in urban areas differ from those in small towns? Why are people more likely to snatch purses on city streets that they are on small-town streets?

❑ Have you ever had your wallet or purse stolen as you walked down the street? Did you see the person who did it? Describe him or her to your classmate(s). What did you do? Did you ever recover your possessions?

❑ Have you ever saved your money for something that you wanted badly? Did it seem like it took forever to save up to buy it? Were you tempted to find a quicker way to get it? What possibilities did you consider?

Thank You, Ma'm

Langston Hughes

She was a large woman with a large purse that had everything in it but a hammer and nails. It had a long strap, and she carried it slung across her shoulder. It was about eleven o'clock at night, dark, and she was walking alone, when a boy ran up behind her and tried *to snatch* her purse. The strap broke with

---

to snatch — to steal

the sudden single *tug* the boy gave it from behind. But the boy's weight and the weight of the purse combined caused him to lose his balance. Instead of taking off *full blast* as he had hoped, the boy fell on his back on the sidewalk and his legs flew up. The large woman simply turned around and kicked him right square in his *blue-jeaned sitter*. Then she reached down, picked the boy up by his shirt front, and shook him until his teeth *rattled*.

2   After that the woman said, "Pick up my pocketbook, boy, and give it here."

3   She still held him tightly. But she bent down enough to permit him to *stoop* and pick up her purse. Then she said, "Now ain't you ashamed of yourself?"

Firmly *gripped* by his shirt front, the boy said, "Yes'm."

The woman said, "What did you want to do it for?"

The boy said, "I didn't *aim to*."

4   By that time two or three people passed, stopped, turned to look, and some stood watching.

"If I turn you loose, will you run?" asked the woman.

"Yes'm," said the boy.

"Then I won't turn you loose," said the woman. She did not release him.

"Lady, I'm sorry," whispered the boy.

"Um-hum! Your face is dirty. *I got a great mind* to wash your face for you. Ain't you got nobody home to tell you to wash your face?"

"No'm," said the boy.

---

tug — pull
full blast — quickly
blue-jeaned sitter — "Sitter" means bottom or buttocks. This boy's bottom was covered by his denim pants — "blue-jeans."
rattled — made a series of sharp, short sounds
stoop — bend forward
gripped — grasped, held tightly
aim to — plan to do it
I got a great mind — I have a strong desire.

"Then it will get washed this evening," said the large woman, starting up the street, *dragging* the frightened boy behind her.

5   He looked as if he were fourteen or fifteen, *frail* and *willow-wild* in tennis shoes and blue jeans.

6   The woman said, "You ought to be my son. I would teach you right from wrong. Least I can do right now is to wash your face. Are you hungry?"

"No'm," said the being-dragged boy. "I just want you to turn me loose."

"Was I bothering you when I turned that corner?" asked the woman.

"No'm."

"But you put yourself in contact with me," said the woman. "If you think that the contact is not going to last awhile, *you got another thought coming.* When I *get through* with you, sir, you are going to remember Mrs. Luella Bates Washington Jones."

7   Sweat popped out on the boy's face and he began to struggle. Mrs. Jones stopped, *jerked him around* in front of her, put a *half-nelson* about his neck, and continued to drag him up the street. When she got to her door, she dragged the boy inside, down a hall, and into a large *kitchenette-furnished room* at the rear of the house. She switched on the light and left the door open. The boy could hear other roomers laughing and talking in the large house. Some of their doors were open, too, so he knew he and the woman were not alone. The woman still had him by the neck in the middle of her room.

---

dragging — pulling
frail — weak
willow-wild — like a willow (a graceful tree that bends easily); slender
you got another thought coming — you had better think again
get through — finish
jerked him around — twisted him around with sharp movements
half-nelson — a strong grip
kitchenette-furnished room — a room with a small kitchen and some furniture

8   She said, "What is your name?"

"Roger," answered the boy;

"Then, Roger, you go to that sink and wash your face," said the woman, *whereupon* she turned him loose — at last. Roger looked at the door — looked at the woman — looked at the door — and went to the sink.

"Let the water run until it gets warm," she said. "Here's a clean towel."

"You *gonna* take me to jail?" asked the boy, bending over the sink.

"Not with that face, I would not take you nowhere," said the woman. "Here I am trying to get home to cook me a bite to eat, and you snatch my pocketbook! Maybe you ain't been to your supper either, late as it be. Have you?"

9   "There's nobody home at my house," said the boy.

"Then we'll eat," said the woman, "I believe you're hungry — or been hungry — to try to snatch my pocketbook!"

"I want a pair of *blue suede shoes*," said the boy.

"Well, you didn't have to snatch my pocketbook to get some suede shoes," said Mrs. Luella Bates Washington Jones. "You could of asked me."

"Ma'm?"

10   The water dripping from his face, the boy looked at her. There was along pause. A very long pause. After he had dried his face and not knowing what else to do, dried it again, the boy turned around, wondering what next. The door was open. He would make a dash for it down the hall. He would run, run, run!

11   The woman was sitting on the *day bed*. After a while, she said, "I were young once and I wanted things I could not get."

---

whereupon — at that moment
gonna — going to
suede shoes — fancy shoes
day bed — A couch that can be converted into a bed.

12   There was another long pause. The boy's mouth opened. Then he *frowned*, not knowing he frowned.

13   The woman said, "Um-hum! You thought I was going to say but, didn't you? You thought I was going to say, but I didn't snatch people's pocketbooks. Well, I wasn't going to say that." Pause. Silence. "I have done things, too, which I would not tell you, son — neither tell God, if He didn't already know. Everybody's got something in common. Sit you down while I fix us something to eat. You might run that comb through your hair so you will look presentable."

14   In another corner of the room behind a screen was a gas plate and an icebox. Mrs. Jones got up and went behind the screen. The woman did not watch the boy to see if he was going to run now, nor did she watch her purse, which she left behind her on the day bed. But the boy *took care* to sit on the far side of the room, away from the purse, where he thought she could easily see him out of the corner of her eye if she wanted to. He did not trust the woman to trust him. And *he did not trust the woman not to trust him.* And he did not want to be mistrusted now.

15   "Do you need somebody to go to the store," asked the boy, "maybe to get some milk or something?"

16   "Don't believe I do," said the woman, "unless you just want sweet milk yourself. I was going to make cocoa out of this canned milk I got here."

17   She heated some *lima beans* and ham she had in the icebox, made the cocoa, and set the table. The woman did not ask the boy anything about where he lived, or his folks, or anything else that would *embarrass* him. Instead, as they ate, she told him about her son in a hotel beauty shop that stayed open late, what

---

frowned — looked with disapproval
took care — was careful
He did not trust the woman not to trust him — He wanted her to trust him.
lima beans — broad, flat, light green beans
embarrass — shame

the work was like, and how all kinds of women came in and out, blondes, redheads and Spanish. Then she cut him half of her ten-cent cake.

"Eat some more, son," she said.

18   When they finished eating, she got up and said, "Now here, take this ten dollars and buy yourself some blue suede shoes. And, next time, do not make the mistake of *latching onto* my pocketbook nor nobody else's — because shoes got by *devilish ways* will burn your feet. I got to get my rest now. But from *here on in*, son, I hope you will behave yourself."

19   She led the way down the hall to the front door and opened it. "Good night! Behave yourself, boy!" she said, looking into the street as he went down the steps.

20   The boy wanted to say something other than "Thank you, ma'm," to Mrs. Luella Bates Washington Jones, but although his lips moved, he couldn't even say that, as he turned at the foot of the *barren stoop* and looked up at the large woman in the door. He barely managed to say, "Thank you," before she shut the door. And he never saw her again.

---

latching onto — trying to take
devilish ways — dishonest ways
here on in — from now on
barren stoop — empty front porch

EXERCISES

Exercise A: Recalling the Reading

Read each statement below and decide whether it is *true* or *false*. If the statement is false, correct it to make a true statement.

1. Mrs. Jones was a large woman.
2. Roger's meeting with Mrs. Jones was friendly from the first.
3. Roger was about ten years old.
4. Roger told Mrs. Jones he was sorry.
5. Roger's meeting with Mrs. Jones took place in the morning.
6. Roger's mother was at home, but his father wasn't.
7. Mrs. Jones lived in a large apartment.
8. Roger was hungry.
9. Mrs. Jones didn't have any children of her own.
10. Mrs. Jones gave Roger ten dollars.

Exercise B: Understanding the Reading

Summarize the main idea.

1. Quickly read the entire story again. In one sentence, tell your classmates why Mrs. Jones invited the boy to dinner.

2. Identify the person(s) or thing(s) referred to in each phrase. Pay special attention to the words in **boldface**.
   a. "... simply turned around and kicked **him** right square in **his** blue-jeaned sitter."
   b. "Now ain't **you** ashamed of **yourself**?"
   c. "Lady, **I'm** sorry, ..."
   d. "But **you** put **yourself** in contact with me ..."
   e. "**You** gonna take me to jail?"
   f. "**You** could of asked me."
   g. "... would make a dash for **it** down the hall."
   h. "**I** have done things, too, ..."
   i. "**I** got to get **my** rest now."
   j. "... **he** couldn't even say that ..."

Exercise C: Analyzing Ideas

Choose correct statements to complete the sentences below. There may be more than one answer for some sentences.

1. Mrs. Jones was a(n) _____ woman.
   a. selfish   b. kind   c. unkind

2. Mrs. Jones was interested in
   a. finding out who Roger's parents were.
   b. punishing Roger for trying to take her purse.
   c. helping Roger change his ways.

3. Roger was
   a. an experienced criminal.
   b. not very experienced at stealing purses.
   c. an excellent purse snatcher.

4. Put the following sentences in order according to the sequence of action in the story.
   a. Roger washed his face.
   b. Mrs. Jones dragged Roger down the street.
   c. Mrs. Jones asked Roger his name.
   d. Mrs. Jones took Roger to her room.

5. Roger tried to snatch Mrs. Jones's pocketbook because
   a. he wanted to buy something for his dinner.
   b. his parents needed the money.
   c. he wanted to buy some shoes.

6. Roger didn't run out of Mrs. Jones's room because
   a. he liked her.
   b. he was afraid she would catch him.
   c. there were other tenants in the house.

7. Mrs. Jones
   a. had a lot of money.
   b. was extremely poor.
   c. didn't have a lot of money.

8. Mrs. Jones had _____ when she was younger.
   a. never stolen anything
   b. been in jail
   c. done some bad things

9. Mrs. Jones left her purse on the bed because
   a. she forgot about it.
   b. she was trying to punish Roger.
   c. she wanted Roger to know she trusted him.

10. Roger wanted to
   a. thank Mrs. Jones.
   b. leave without saying anything.
   c. say something more than thank you.

Exercise D: Word Study: Part One

Get and its uses

The verb *get* appears frequently in informal speech in American English. It has many different meanings, including the following: *must* (have to), *obtain, buy, receive, have* (possess), *be able to, become.* Read each sentence below; then rewrite the sentences, substituting one of the words listed for the verb *get.*

1. I've *got* a cold.

_____

2. I was going to wear the dress I've *got* in the closet.

_____

3. I've *got* to go now.

_____

4. Shall I *get* you some milk at the store?

_____

5. Where did you *get* your book?

_____

6. When will you *get* to take your vacation?

_____

7. It's *getting* late.

_____

8. When do you *get* your paycheck?

_____

9. I couldn't *get* all the things I wanted.

_____

10. I *got* that letter this morning.

_____

Exercise D: Word Study: Part Two

Infinitives and their uses

Langston Hughes uses infinitives in two different ways in this story: 1) as *verb completers*, and 2) as a way to express *purpose*.

Examples of 1:

> We want *to eat* dinner.

> We hope *to leave* soon.

Example of 2:

> I stopped *to say* hello. (Meaning: I stopped in order to say hello.)

Complete the sentences below, using information from the story, "Thank You, M'am." Write the number (1) or (2) after each sentence to show which way the infinitive is used.

1. Roger wanted to buy _a pair of blue suede shoes._   (1)

2. Mrs. Jones took Roger home _____ . ( )

3. Mrs. Jones reached down _____ . ( )

4. Roger did't have anybody at home to tell him_____
    _____ . ( )

5. He went to the sink _____ . ( )

6. Mrs. Jones let Roger loose _____ . ( )

7. Mrs. Jones went behind the screen_____ . ( )

Exercise E: Structure and Style: Part One

Find the sentences in Column A in the text of the story. Match them to their Standard English meanings in Column B.

Column A	Column B
____ **1.** I didn't aim to.	**a.** If I let you go —
____ **2.** I've got a great mind to —	**b.** You had better think again.
____ **3.** If I turn you loose —	**c.** From now on —
____ **4.** From here on in —	**d.** I have a strong desire to —
____ **5.** You got another thought coming.	**e.** I didn't intend to.
____ **6.** — got by devilish ways	**f.** Nor would I tell—
____ **7.** Neither tell	**g.** — obtained dishonestly

Exercise E: Structure and Style: Part Two

One of the dialects of English is Black English. It is an informal way of speaking used among many African Americans when they are among friends or at home. One of the ways in which this dialect is different from Standard English is in the use of verb forms.

Black English	**Standard English**
he/she *do*	he/she *does*
he/she *don't*	he/she *doesn't*
I/you/we/they *is*	I/you/we/they *are*
he/she *be*	he/she *is*
we/you/they *be*	we/you/they *are*
I *ain't*	I'm *not*
I *ain't got no* pencils	I *don't have any* pencils
I *were*	I *was*
he/she *gonna*	he/she's *going to*

Read the sentences in Black English below and rewrite them using Standard English forms.

1. Ain't you got nobody home?

_____

2. Late as it be

_____

3. Maybe you ain't been to your supper.

_____

4. I were young once

_____

5. You is gonna remember me.

_____

6. He don't know better.

_____

7. We is gonna eat dinner now.

_____

Exercise F: Questions for Discussion or Writing

1. When Mrs. Jones lets Roger free, he can run away or go wash his face at the sink. Why does he obey her instead of running away?
2. Explain Mrs. Jones's statement: "Everybody's got something in common."
3. Why can't Roger say anything when he leaves Mrs. Jones? Have you ever been speechless when you've wanted to say a lot of things?
4. Does Roger's character change from the beginning of the story to the end of the story? If so, how?
5. Close your book and think about this story. Then write answers to these questions:
   a. Why did the boy try to snatch Mrs. Jones's pocketbook?
   b. Why did Mrs. Jones invite him to have supper in her house?
   c. Why didn't the boy take the woman's purse from her day bed?
   d. Why didn't the woman ask the boy about where he lived or his folks?
   e. Why did Roger have so much difficulty saying "thank you" to Mrs. Jones?

6. We know how "Thank You, Ma'm" ends: Roger can barely thank Mrs. Jones. Imagine another ending. One week later, Roger returns to see Mrs. Jones. He is wearing a new pair of blue suede shoes. He is carrying a large grocery bag. He knocks on the door.

Mrs. Jones: _____

Roger: It's me, Roger.

Mrs. Jones: _____

Roger: I come to see you. Ain't you gonna let me in?

Mrs. Jones (opens the door and looks at Roger carefully):
              Well, look at you, wearing your blue suede
              shoes. What you got in the bag?

Roger: _____

Mrs. Jones: Well, ain't that nice. Come on in and I'll fix us a
             bite to eat.

Roger (enters Mrs. Jones's room and puts down the bag of
       groceries):

             Thank you, ma'm. And I want to give you
             something else.

Mrs. Jones: What's that, son?

Roger: (holds out a ten-dollar bill):

             I got to pay you back, ma'm.

Mrs. Jones: _____

LESSON 8

You Go Your Way,
I'll Go Mine

The Writer

WILLIAM SAROYAN (1908 – 1981)

William Saroyan was a native Californian of Armenian descent who grew up in the San Joaquin Valley near Fresno. As a young man he decided to be a writer; he used some of his painful and funny experiences as plots for his early stories.

"You Go Your Way, I'll Go Mine" is taken from *The Human Comedy*, a novel Saroyan wrote in 1943 during the Second World War. It is about ordinary people in a small California town trying to understand and manage their lives as fear and death touch them.

The Reading

After the Great Depression (1930-1937), America became involved in the Second World War (1939 to 1945). America entered the war in 1941, after the Japanese bombed Pearl Harbor in Hawaii. The war in Europe ended when the Italians and Germans surrendered to the Allied forces in the summer of 1945. The war in Asia ended after American forces dropped an atomic bomb on Hiroshima in August 1945.

It was the custom of the War Department of the United States government to notify the survivors of American soldiers who had been killed in battle or were missing in action. Hundreds of thousands of telegrams were sent. In big cities where telephones were plentiful, telephone operators read the telegrams to survivors. In small towns, like the one in Saroyan's story, telegrams were delivered directly to survivors. The "messenger boys," as they were called, were usually teenagers who rode bicycles to make their deliveries.

SHARING EXPERIENCES

Compare your responses with those of your classmates.

❑ Is the style of writing used in a telegram different from a letter writing style? If so, how and why is it different?

❑ Have you ever received a telegram? If so, was the message good or bad news? How did you feel when the telegram was delivered? How was it delivered?

❑ Have you ever sent a telegram? If so, what kind of news were you sending? Are many telegrams sent these days? Why/why not? What forms of communication have replaced telegrams?

❑ Has anyone in your family been killed in a war? Who was it? How did your family receive the news?

❑ How do communities in your country remember their men and women who died as soldiers in wars? Do they hold a ceremony or a religious service? What do they do for the families of the dead soldiers?

❑ There are lots of Spanish-speaking people in the United States. Many are from Mexico. In which states do most of them live? Do most of them learn English quickly? Why or why not?

❑ Share what you know about people from Mexico. Describe relationships between parents and children in this culture.

You Go Your Way, I'll Go Mine

William Saroyan

The *messenger* got off his bicycle in front of the house of Mrs. Rosa Sandoval. He went to the door and knocked gently. He knew almost immediately that someone was inside the house. He could not hear anything, but he was sure the knock was bringing someone to the door and he was most eager to see who this person would be — this woman named Rosa Sandoval who was now to hear of murder in the world and to feel it in

---

messenger — a person employed to carry telegrams, letters or parcels

herself. The door was not a long time opening, but there was no hurry in the way it moved on its *hinges*. The movement of the door was as if, whoever she was, had nothing in the world to fear. Then the door was open, and there she was.

2   To Homer the Mexican woman was beautiful. He could see that she had been patient all her life, so that now, after years of it, her lips were set in a gentle and saintly smile. But like all people who never receive telegrams the appearance of a messenger at the front door is full of terrible *implications*. Homer knew that Mrs. Rosa Sandoval was shocked to see him. Her first word was the first word of all surprise. She said "Oh," as if instead of a messenger she had thought of opening the door to someone she had known a long time and would be pleased to sit down with. Before she spoke again she studied Homer's eyes and Homer knew that she knew the message was not a welcome one.

"You have a telegram?" she said.

3   It wasn't Homer's fault. His work was to deliver telegrams. Even so, it seemed to him that he was part of the whole mistake. He felt *awkward* and almost as if he alone were responsible for what had happened. At the same time he wanted to *come right out and say*, "I'm only a messenger, Mrs. Sandoval. I'm very sorry I must bring you a telegram like this, but it is only because it is my work to do so."

4   "Who is it for?" the Mexican woman said.

"Mrs. Rosa Sandoval, 1129 G Street," Homer said. He *extended* the telegram to the Mexican woman, but she would not touch it.

"Are you Mrs. Sandoval?" Homer said.

"Please," the woman said. "Please come in. I cannot read English. I am Mexican. I read only 'La Prensa' which comes

---

hinges — metal plates that fasten a door to a frame
implications — possibilities
awkward — uncomfortable
to come right out and say — say directly
extended — handed

from Mexico City." She paused a moment and looked at the boy standing awkwardly as near the door as he could be and still be inside the house.

5   But now the woman interrupted him. "But you must open the telegram and read it to me," she said. "You have not opened it."

"Yes, ma'am," Homer said as if he were speaking to a school teacher who had just corrected him.

He opened the telegram with nervous fingers. The Mexican woman *stooped* to pick up the torn envelope, and tried to smooth it out. As she did so she said, "Who sent the telegram — my son Juan Domingo?"

"No, ma'am," Homer said. "The telegram is from the War Department."

"War Department?" the Mexican woman said.

"Mrs. Sandoval," Homer said swiftly, "your son is dead. Maybe it's a mistake. Everybody makes a mistake, Mrs. Sandoval. Maybe it wasn't your son. Maybe it was somebody else. The telegram *says* it was Juan Domingo. But maybe the telegram is wrong."

6   The Mexican woman pretended not to hear.

"Oh, do not be afraid," she said. "Come inside. Come inside. I will bring you candy." She took the boy's arm and brought him to the table at the center of the room and there she *made him sit*.

"All boys like candy," she said. "I will bring you candy."

Homer took a piece of candy from the box, put it into his mouth, and tried to chew.

"You would not bring me a bad telegram," she said. "You are a good boy — like my little Juanito when he was a little boy. Eat another piece." And she made the messenger take another piece of the candy.

---

stooped — bent over
says — reports
made him sit — put him in a chair

7   Homer sat chewing the dry candy while the Mexican woman talked. "It is our own candy," she said, "from *cactus*." I made it for my Juanito when he come home, but you eat it. You are my boy, too."

8   Now suddenly she began to *sob, holding herself in* as if *weeping* were a *disgrace*. Homer wanted to *get up* and run, but he knew he would stay. He just didn't know what else to do to try to make the woman less unhappy, and if she had asked him to take the place of her son, *he would not have been able to refuse*, because he would not have known how. He got to his feet, as if by standing he meant to begin correcting what could not be corrected and then he knew the *foolishness* of his *intention* and became more awkward than ever. In his heart he was saying over and over again, "What can I do? What the hell can I do? I'm only the messenger."

---

cactus — a desert plant
sob — cry heavily
holding herself in — trying not to cry
weeping — crying
disgrace — shameful
get up — stand up
he would not have been able to refuse — he could not have said no
foolishness — silliness, uselessness
intention — plan

EXERCISES

Exercise A: Recalling the Reading

Read each statement and decide whether it is *true* or *false*. If the statement is false, correct it to make a true statement.

1. Homer's work was to deliver telegrams.
2. Homer could not tell if anyone was home when he knocked at the door.
3. Mrs. Sandoval received many telegrams.
4. Mrs. Sandoval couldn't read English.
5. The telegram was from Mrs. Sandoval's son.
6. Mrs. Sandoval was expecting her son Juan Domingo to come home.
7. Homer didn't want to give Mrs. Sandoval the news about her son.
8. Mrs. Sandoval gave Homer an enchilada.
9. Homer didn't want to stay at Mrs. Sandoval's house.
10. Homer stayed with Mrs. Sandoval because he felt so comfortable in her house.

Exercise B: Understanding the Reading

Summarize the main idea.

1. Quickly read the entire story again. In one sentence, tell your classmates why Mrs. Sandoval asked Homer to sit down and have some candy

2. Identify the person(s) or thing(s) referred to in each phrase. Pay special attention to the words in **boldface**.
   a. "**He** could not hear anything . . ."
   b. "**Her** first word was the first word of all surprise."
   c. "Even so, it seemed to **him** that **he** was part of the whole mistake."
   d. "**I** read only *La Prensa* which comes from Mexico City."
   e. "**Who** sent the telegram . . . ?"

f. "**Everybody** makes a mistake . . ."
g. "Oh, do not be afraid . . ."
h. "**You** are my boy, too."
i. ". . . wanted to get up and run . . ."
j. "**I'm** only the messenger."

Exercise C: Analyzing Ideas

Choose correct statements to complete the sentences below.

1. When Homer knocked at the door to Mrs. Rosa Sandoval's house,
    a. he knew that no one would be at home.
    b. he was eager to see who Mrs. Sandoval was.
    c. he didn't know anything about the contents of the telegram.

2. ". . . this woman named Rosa Sandoval who was now to hear of murder in the world and to feel it in herself," refers to
    a. the news in the telegram.
    b. Homer's apologies to Mrs. Sandoval.
    c. a story in the newspaper.

3. Homer felt _____ about delivering the telegram to Mrs. Sandoval.
    a. awkward and apologetic
    b. confident and blameless
    c. indifferent and angry

4. Mrs. Sandoval
    a. didn't have any idea what was in the telegram.
    b. knew that the message was not a welcome one.
    c. was expecting good news in the telegram.

5. To Homer, the Mexican woman was
   a. beautiful and patient.
   b. unattractive and impatient.
   c. charming and impatient.

6. Before he opened the telegram, Homer
   a. didn't know what news was in it.
   b. wondered what news was in it.
   c. knew what news was in it.

7. Homer read the telegram to Mrs. Sandoval because
   a. he wanted to.
   b. she couldn't read English.
   c. she was crying and couldn't read it.

8. Referring to the story again, put the following statements in the order of the action in the story:
   a. Mr. Sandoval began to sob.
   b. Homer took a piece of candy from the box.
   c. Homer read the telegram to Mrs. Sandoval.
   d. Mrs. Sandoval said to Homer, "Oh, do not be afraid. . . ."

9. Homer knew he would stay with Mrs. Sandoval awhile because
   a. he wanted to make her less unhappy.
   b. he didn't want to leave.
   c. he wanted to be her son.

Exercise D: Word Study: Part One

Verbs in different contexts

These common English verbs in your reading can have a number of different meanings, depending on the context of the sentences in which they are used: *study, say, feel, open, make*. Read each sentence below and fill in the space with the verb which best completes the meaning of the sentence. Note tense changes that may be necessary.

    study   make   say   feel   open

1. Don't you _____ well today? Your face is very pale.

2. The door _____ very slowly.

3. She didn't _____ very hard last semester, so her grades were not high.

4. What does the letter _____ ?

5. She _____ his eyes carefully and concluded that he had bad news for her.

6. She _____ her own wedding dress.

7. The baby's forehead _____ hot, so his mother knew that he had a fever.

8. "It's our own candy," she said. "We _____ it from cactus."

9. I would like to _____ a checking account at that bank.

10. He wanted to come right out and _____ , "I'm not responsible for this."

11. She was so tired that she could barely keep her eyes _____ .

12. She _____ him eat another piece of candy.

13. He _____ the telegram with nervous fingers.

14. He _____ the contract carefully before signing it.

15. He _____ very awkward standing there after everyone had gone.

Exercise D: Word Study: Part Two

Verb 1 and Verb 2

1. In English, we use a small group of verbs again and again: *can/could, shall/should, will/would, may/might, have to/ought to,* and *must.* We call these verbs *modals,* and we add them to other verbs like this:

> "Homer *could* not *hear* anything . . ."
> "He *could see* that she had been patient. . . ."

Notice that *hear* and *see* are infinitives (*to hear, to see*), but the word *to* is missing when the *modals* are used.

2. We also add verbs to verbs in another way.

> "Homer *wanted to* get up and run. . . ."
> "The Mexican woman *pretended* not *to hear*."

Notice that when we use the verbs *want, try, learn, agree, like, need*, and other verbs like them, the infinitives (*to get up; to hear*) that follow those verbs keep the word *to*.

3. Using information from the story, complete as many of these sentences as you can by adding verbs to verbs.

   a. I'm very sorry I must _____ you a telegram like this.

   b. Mrs. Sandoval stooped _____ the envelope.

   c. She tried _____ the torn envelope.

   d. You would not _____ me a bad telegram.

   e. Homer wanted _____ her the truth.

   f. You _____ open the telegram.

   g. Homer tried _____ the candy.

   h. Homer knew he _____ stay.

   i. Homer wanted _____ something, but he _____ not.

   j. Mrs. Sandoval wanted Homer _____ the place of her son.

Exercise E: Questions for Discussion and Writing

1. What do you think the title of this story means?
2. Why does Homer read the telegram to Mrs. Sandoval?
3. Why does Mrs. Sandoval do the following things after hearing the news of her son's death?
   a. pretends not to hear.
   b. tells Homer to come inside.

    c. makes Homer eat some candy.

    d. tells Homer that he is her boy, too.

    e. acts ashamed of her sobbing.

4. Does Homer understand Mrs. Sandoval's sadness? Find phrases from the story to support your answer.

5. How did the story end? Would you have stayed, if you had been in Homer's place? Did Homer stay at Mrs. Sandoval's very long?

6. When you have important news for people in your family or for your friends, do you prefer to call them on the telephone, send them a telegram, or send them a letter? Explain why. Compare your answers with those of your classmates.

3

Memories

LESSON 9

Antonio's First Day of School

The Writer

RUDOLFO ANAYA (1937 –   )

Rudolfo Anaya is a native of New Mexico. He has two graduate degrees from the University of New Mexico and has been working in the schools of New Mexico for many years. In 1971, he won a special literary award which is given only to Mexican-American authors. This prize was given to him for his novel *Bless Me, Ultima*, from which the reading below is taken.

Anaya writes, he says, to reflect on the people that he met, heard, and saw while growing up in New Mexico. He also wants his readers to understand the special beauty of the environment of his native state. Much of his writing is autobiographical. In the reading below, he talks about his first day at the English-speaking public school.

The Reading

"Antonio's First Day of School" is a story told by a young boy from a Hispanic — that is, Spanish-speaking and Spanish cultural — background. This boy, Antonio Marez, is a first-grader, perhaps six or seven years old, and like most children, he misses his mother that first day of school.

Antonio's feelings of difference — in language, in food, in appearance — and strangeness are the problems in this story. How Antonio overcomes these feelings is the moral of the story.

SHARING EXPERIENCES

Compare your responses with those of your classmates.

❏ Recall your first day of school. How did you feel when you woke up in the morning — sick, anxious, excited, fearful? Who woke you up? How did you get to school? Did you walk, ride a bus, or were you driven in a car? How did you feel when you first saw the school building, your classroom, your teacher(s) and your classmates?

❏ Have you attended a school (or workplace) where you felt different because of your language, clothes, social status, or customs? Did you feel lonely? Did anyone help you? How did you overcome your loneliness? What did you do at lunch time?

❏ How do you communicate with people if you can't speak their language? Can you tell if someone is trying to help you, even if you don't understand the words?

❏ Find New Mexico on a map of the United States. What do you know about this state? Look at some travel pictures about the state. Do you know of other places with similar landscape?

❏ Some Mexican-Americans are migrant workers. They harvest agricultural crops in the western and the southwestern United States. The families move from one state to another as each crop comes into season. As a result, the children have to enter a new school every two or three months. How would going to three or more schools each year affect a child?

Antonio's First Day of School

Rudolfo Anaya

On the first day of school I awoke with a sick feeling in my stomach. It did not hurt; it just made me feel weak. The sun did not sing as it came over the hill. Today I would take the goat path and *trek* into town for years and years of *schooling*. For the first time I would be away from the protection of my mother. I was excited and sad about it.

2   Somehow I got to the *school grounds*, but I was lost. The school was larger than I had expected. Its *huge, yawning doors were menacing*. I looked for my sisters, but every face I saw

---

trek — walk
schooling — education
school grounds — the land around the school
huge, yawning doors were menacing — large open doors looked dangerous

was strange. I looked again at the doors of the *sacred* halls, but I was too afraid to enter. My mother had said to go to Miss Maestas, but I did not know where to begin to find her. I had come to the town, and I had come to school, and I was very lost and afraid in the nervous, excited *swarm of kids*.

3   It was then that I felt a hand on my shoulder. I turned and looked into the eyes of a strange red-haired boy. He spoke English, a *foreign tongue*.

4   "First grade," was all I could answer. He smiled and took my hand, and with him I entered school. The building was *cavernous* and dark. It had strange, unfamiliar smells and *sounds that seemed to gurgle* from its belly. There was a big hall and many rooms, and many mothers with children passed in and out of the rooms.

5   I wished for my mother, but I put away the thought because I knew I was expected to become a man. A *radiator snapped with steam* and I jumped. The red-haired boy laughed and led me into one of the rooms. This room was brighter than the hall. So it was like this that I entered school.

6   Miss Maestas was a kind woman. She thanked the boy whose name was Red for bringing me in and then asked my name. I told her I did not speak English.

"*Como te llamas?*" she asked.

"Antonio Marez," I replied. I told her my mother said I should see her and that my mother sent her *regards*.

She smiled. "Anthony Marez," she wrote in a book. I *drew closer* to look at the letters formed by her pen. "Do you want to learn to write?" she asked. "Yes," I answered.

---

sacred — serious-looking
swarm of kids — large group of children
foreign tongue — a foreign language
cavernous — extremely large
sounds that seemed to gurgle — low, bubbling sounds
radiator — machine used to heat a room
snapped with steam — made a sudden sharp noise
como te llamas? — Spanish for "What's your name?"
regards — greetings
drew closer — came closer

"Good," she smiled.

7   I was *fascinated* by the black letters that formed on the paper and made my name. Miss Maestas gave me a crayon and some paper and I sat in the corner *copying my name over and over.* She was very busy the rest of the day with the other children that came to the room. Many cried when their mothers left. I sat in my corner alone and wrote. By noon I could write my name, and when Miss Maestas discovered that, she was very pleased.

8   She took me to the front of the room and spoke to the other boys and girls. She pointed at me but I did not understand her. Then the other boys and girls laughed and pointed at me. I did not feel so good. *Thereafter,* I kept away from the groups as much as I could and worked alone. I worked hard. I listened to the strange sounds. I learned new names, new words.

9   At noon we opened our lunches to eat. Miss Maestas left the room and a high school girl came and sat at the desk while we ate. My mother had *packed* a small jar of hot beans and some good, green chile wrapped in *tortillas.* When the other children saw my lunch, they laughed and pointed again. Even the high school girl laughed. They showed me their sandwiches which were made of bread. Again I did not feel well.

10   I *gathered* my lunch and *slipped out* of the room. The strangeness of the school and the other children made me very sad. I did not understand them. I *sneaked* around the back of the school building, and standing against the wall I tried to eat. But I couldn't. A huge lump seemed to form in my throat and tears came to my eyes. I *yearned* for my mother and at the same time

---

fascinated — very interested
copying my name over and over — writing my name many times
thereafter — after that
packed — put into a bag
tortillas — flat corn "'pancakes"
gathered — picked up
slipped out — walked out quietly
sneaked — walked carefully, unnoticed by anyone
yearned — wanted very much

I understood that she had sent me to this place where I was an *outcast*. I had tried hard to learn and they had laughed at me. I had opened my lunch to eat and again they had laughed and pointed at me.

11   The pain and sadness seemed to *spread to my soul* and I felt for the first time what the *grown-ups* call, *la tristeza de la vida*. I wanted to run away, to hide, to run and never come back, never see anyone again. But I knew that if I did I would *shame my family name*, that my mother's dream would *crumble*. I knew I had to grow up and be a man, but oh it was so very hard.

12   But no, I was not alone. Down the wall near the corner I saw two other boys who had sneaked out of the room. They were big boys. I knew they were from the farms of Delia. We *banded together* and in our *union* found strength. We found a few others who were like us, different in language and customs, and part of our loneliness was gone. When the winter *set in* we moved into the auditorium and there, although many a meal was eaten in complete silence, we felt we belonged. We *struggled against* the feeling of loneliness that *gnawed at our souls* and we *overcame* it; that feeling I never shared again with anyone.

---

outcast — someone who is different from everybody else
spread to my soul — felt in my entire body
grown-ups — adults
la tristeza de la vida — Spanish for "life's sadness"
shame my family name — make people lose respect for my family
crumble — break into small pieces
banded together — joined together
union — group
set in — came
struggled against — fought against
gnawed at our souls — made our entire body feel bad (literally, to bite at and wear down or make weak)
overcame — got rid of

EXERCISES

Exercise A: Recalling the Reading

Read each statement below and tell whether it is *true* or *false*. If the statement is false, correct it to make a true statement.

1. Antonio was excited about his first day at school.
2. Antonio's sisters took him to the school building.
3. Antonio knew the red-haired boy.
4. Antonio did not know how to speak English.
5. Miss Maestas didn't know how to speak Spanish.
6. Antonio practiced writing his name all morning on the first day of school.
7. All the children had lunches like Antonio's.
8. Antonio was very sad because the other children laughed at him.
9. Antonio didn't want to shame the family name.
10. Antonio ate his lunch alone every school day.

Exercise B: Understanding the Reading

Summarize the main idea.

1. Quickly read the entire story again. In one sentence, tell your classmates why Antonio went outside to eat his lunch.
2. Identify the person(s) or thing(s) referred to in each phrase. Pay special attention to the words in **boldface**.
   a. "For the first time **I** would be away from the protection of my mother."
   b. "**Its** huge, yawning doors were menacing."
   c. "**He** spoke English, a foreign tongue."
   d. "**It** had strange, unfamiliar smells and sounds that seemed to gurgle from **its** belly."
   e. ". . . laughed and led **me** into one of the rooms."
   f. "Do **you** want to learn to write?"
   g. "**Many** cried when their mothers left."
   h. ". . . laughed and pointed at me."

   i. "I yearned for . . . , and at the same time I understood that **she** had sent me to this place where I was an out-cast."

   j. "But **I** knew that if **I** did **I** would shame my family name, . . ."

Exercise C: Analyzing Ideas

Choose correct statements to complete the sentences below.

1. Antonio had a sick feeling in his stomach when he awoke because
   a. he had eaten something which had made him sick.
   b. he was leaving his mother's protection for the first time.
   c. he didn't want to walk all the way to school.

2. Antonio was _____ when he got to the school grounds.
   a. happy and excited   c. lost and nervous
   b. calm and bored

3. The red-haired boy
   a. was a stranger who helped Antonio.
   b. was a friend who spoke Spanish.
   c. was a stranger who spoke Spanish.

4. Antonio didn't think about his mother because
   a. he was expected to be a man.
   b. he was very busy getting used to the school.
   c. the other children laughed at him.

5. Miss Maestas
   a. didn't speak Spanish to Antonio because she wanted him to learn English.
   b. spoke Spanish to Antonio because he didn't speak English.
   c. didn't speak Spanish to Antonio because she didn't know the language.

6. Antonio was left sitting in the corner of the room copying his name because
   a. Miss Maestas didn't want to teach a non-English speaker.
   b. Miss Maestas was busy with the other children.
   c. Antonio didn't want to be with the other children.

7. The other children laughed at Antonio because
   a. he was different from them.
   b. he said things that were very funny.
   c. he was learning to write.

8. Antonio took his lunch out of the classroom because
   a. he was used to eating alone.
   b. the other children laughed at the lunch he brought.
   c. he didn't want to look at the other children's lunches.

9. Antonio felt very sad because
   a. his mother didn't want him to go to school.
   b. he could not eat his lunch.
   c. the school and the other children were strange.

10. Antonio and the other students who were different
    a. overcame some of their loneliness by forming their own group.
    b. never spoke to each other.
    c. were not able to share anything among themselves.

Exercise D: Word Study

1. Notice how two-word modifiers are made.
   i. The boy has red hair. (adjective plus noun)
   ii. The boy is red-haired. (adjective plus verb + *ed*)
   iii. He is a red-haired boy. (two-word adjective modifying a noun)

   Using the process illustrated above, form nine two-word modifiers of your own by combining a word from Column A with a word from Column B. Use a hyphen between the two words. Use any combination of words that makes sense to you. The first one is done for you.

Column A	Column B	New Modifiers
white	leg	white legged
brown	skin	_____
red	face	_____
thin	finger	_____
long	foot	_____
thick	lip	_____
weak	hand	_____
fat	arm	_____
left	hip	_____
black	hair	_____

2. Now use five of the new modifiers in your own sentences:

1. _____

2. _____

3. _____

4. _____

5. _____

Exercise E: Structure and Style

Since the speaker in "Antonio's First Day" is also the main character of the story, we are told how Antonio felt about the events in the story. Below is a list of words describing the various feelings Antonio mentions in the story. Find examples of each of these feelings in the story. Write down the sentence(s) from the story which describe these feelings.

1. sad and excited

_____

2. lost and confused

_____

3. afraid

_____

4. embarrassed

_____

5. lonely

_____

6. a sense of belonging

_____

Exercise F: Questions for Discussion and Writing

1. Throughout the story, Antonio had a conflict. He wanted to run home to his mother's protection, but he also wanted to grow up. Why did he feel like running away from school? Why was it important for him to stay?
2. What did Antonio share with the boys from the farms of Delia? What did they communicate to each other?
3. How did Antonio and the boys behind the school overcome their loneliness? Describe the feeling Antonio had about his group (which he never shared with anyone again).
4. How did Miss Maestas help Antonio? Do you think she understood his problems or not? Explain.
5. Close your book and think about this reading. Explain what this phrase means: "We struggled against the feeling of loneliness that gnawed at our souls, and we overcame it . . ."

Exercise G: Additional Activities

Choose *one* of the topics below.

1. Do you attend a school (a) where English is the native language of most of the students or (b) where most of the

students study English as a foreign language? Can you remember your first day at this school? Talk about it or write about it.

2. Pretend that you are Miss Maestas, Antonio's teacher. Tell what happens in paragraphs 6 and 7 from *her* point of view. You should use the pronoun *I* to report Miss Maestas's words and actions, and use *he* to report the feelings, words, and actions of Antonio.

3. When Antonio came home after his first day at school, he and his mother had this conversation (in Spanish). Supply the missing lines (in English, of course).

Mother: Ah, you're home from school. Why do you look so sad?

Antonio: _____

Mother: Didn't you find Miss Maestas?

Antonio: _____

Mother: Didn't she help you?

Antonio: _____

Mother: The children laughed and pointed at you? Why?

Antonio: I don't know. They did that again at lunchtime — when they saw my lunch.

Mother: _____

Antonio: Bread. Sandwiches. I wanted to run away.

Mother: _____

Antonio: No. I didn't want to _____

_____ .

Mother: Will you go back to _____ ?

Antonio: Yes, because _____

_____ .

LESSON 10

George Washington, My Countryman

The Writer

MARY ANTIN (1881-1949)

As Mary Antin tells us in the reading, she was born in a Russian village. She emigrated to America in 1894, when she was thirteen years old. She attended New York public schools and went on to attend Columbia University and Barnard College in New York City.

Mary Antin wrote *The Promised Land* in 1912. It first appeared as a "serial" (published in monthly installments) in *The Atlantic Monthly*. It was a very much admired chronicle of the lives of European Jews in a new land. The success of *The Promised Land* and the book that followed it, *They Who Knock at Our Gates*, made Mary Antin a popular writer, and she toured America as a lecturer.

The Reading

This reading is from *The Promised Land*. The illustration gives some idea of the time in which Mary Antin's experiences took place: just about the turn of the century; that is, the period between 1895 and 1900.

Mary Antin grew up in a Jewish household. There was a strong belief in creating a homeland for Jews who were scattered around the world. The toast "Next Year in Jerusalem" is a hope and a promise. Today, one hundred years later, there is a Jewish homeland in the state of Israel; and the idea of equality among people of all kinds in America is still strong.

SHARING EXPERIENCES

Compare your responses with those of your classmates.

❑ Explain what is meant by "patriotism." How does a patriot feel about his or her country? What are some examples of patriotic behavior?

❑ Which citizens of your native country do you admire? Why?

❑ Did you study about American history in your country? What did you learn about George Washington? Name other American patriots whom you have studied about.

❑ What kinds of freedoms are guaranteed to citizens of the United States of America? Are these freedoms guaranteed to citizens of your native country?

❑ If you are studying English in the United States or are planning to come to the United States, tell why you came or why you want to come to this country.

George Washington, My Countryman

Mary Antin

We came to America from Russia. The name of our place was Polotzk. Can you say it? It was easy in my language, Russian. "George Washington" is easy in English, but it was hard for me. Every time I tried to say his name I trembled and my voice shook. I felt *humble*. George Washington was a great man. I was just a little girl from Russia.

2   I wanted to know George Washington. I looked at his picture often. Then I closed my eyes, and I could see him with my eyes shut. How could I know this man? How could I speak to him. He was dead. What could I tell him? He never told a

---

humble — unimportant

lie. I had never told a lie, either. He was very brave, but I was not brave. He crossed the Delaware River in a snowstorm. I was afraid to go out when it was snowing. I could never be President of the United States.

3   One day our teacher, Miss Dwight, talked to us about *fellow citizens*. I thought about this idea. In America, you are a *citizen* when you are born here. You can become an American citizen if you were born in another country. My father had become a citizen and I was a citizen, too, because I was his daughter. Then I was a fellow citizen, and George Washington was another! This was a great *discovery*! George Washington was my countryman, and America was my country. The country was for all citizens, and I was a citizen.

4   Why was this discovery so important to me? We were Jews, and Jews in Russia lived *in exile*. We had no flag to love, and we really had no country. We had no heroes, but we had our religion and our hopes. Every year at *Passover* we said, "Next year, may we be in *Jerusalem*." I didn't know that Jerusalem was a real place in the world. When we came to America, I found my Jerusalem. It was Boston. I found my flag. It was the *stars and stripes*. And I found my heroes in the history of America. The greatest hero was my fellow citizen, George Washington.

5   I wanted to tell everyone about my discovery. I *decided* to write a poem in English. I had studied English for less than two years. A poem in English was going to be difficult! I discovered that only one word *rhymed* with "Washington." It was "Washington"! But the poem was in my heart, and I *struggled* until I finished it.

---

lie — something that is not true
fellow citizens — equally important citizens
citizens — a member of society
discovery — fact to learn
in exile — having no country of one's own
Passover — a Jewish holiday
Jerusalem— a city in Israel
stars and stripes — the American flag   **decided** — chose
rhymed — sounded the same   **struggled** — worked very hard

6   I showed my poem to my father. When he read it, tears came to his eyes and his hands trembled as he held my poem. I showed it to my teacher, Mis Dwight. She said many kind things to me. When we *celebrated George Washington's birthday* in class, my teacher asked me to read my poem to the class. I was very happy because at last I could speak to George Washington. But I was frightened. I did not look *heroic*.

7   It was a long poem — twelve *stanzas*. I faced my forty fellow citizens. I stared at their eighty eyes, and I gave it to them, stanza after stanza. Even the bad boys in the back row of the classroom listened quietly. Here are some of the stanzas:

> He whose courage, will, amazing bravery
> Did free his land from a *despot's* rule,
> From man's greatest evil, almost slavery,
> And all that's taught in *tyranny's* school,
> Who gave his land its liberty,
> Who was he?
> 'Twas he who e'er will be our pride,
> Immortal Washington,
> Who always did in truth *confide*.
> We hail our Washington!
> Wrote the famous Constitution;
> Sacred's the hand
> That this blessed guide to man had given which says "One
> And all of mankind are alike, excepting none."
> Then we weary Hebrew children at last found rest
> In the land where *reigned* Freedom, and like a nest
> To homeless birds your land proved to us, and therefore
> Will we gratefully sing your praise evermore.

---

celebrated George Washington's birthday — George Washington's birthday is a special holiday in the United States
heroic — like a hero (such as Washington)
stanzas — the parts of a a poem; a stanza often has many lines
despot — bad ruler
tyranny — bad government
confide — believe
reigned — ruled

8   Other classes in the school asked me to read my poem. Someone — maybe it was my father — told me about the newspaper, the **Boston Transcript**. The newspaper might *print my poem*. I copied my poem very carefully, and then I made a trip to the newspaper office.

9   I got lost on the way. Finally, a *newsboy* helped me, and I found the office of the **Boston Transcript**. Then I got lost again. There were *seven stories* in the building. Where was the editor? Who would print my poem about George Washington? At last, I found the editor's office. I gave him my poem and I asked him to print it. He stared at me and smiled. I felt about *eleven inches high*. My voice got smaller and smaller, and then I stopped talking. No, the paper would not print my poem. . . . I went across the street to the **Boston Herald**. "Yes," said the editor of the *Herald*. "We will print your poem."

10   On the way home, I dreamed. I smiled. Thousands of people would read my poem. They would see my name, and they would *wonder who I was*. "Who is Mary Antin?" they would ask.

11   When the **Boston Herald** printed my poem, my family and I were excited. It looked wonderful, like real poetry. The editor wrote a little story about **me** — Mary Antin. And there was **my** name at the bottom of the poem. My father took all the money in the house. He went out and bought all the **Boston Heralds** he could find. He gave them to our friends. Some of them could read, and some could not, but it didn't matter. My father cut my poem out of the paper. He carried it in his pocket, next to his heart, for a long time. He was very *proud of me*. I was proud too; George Washington was my countryman, my fellow citizen, my hero.

---

print my poem — put in the newspaper
newsboy — someone who sells newspaper
seven stories — seven floors
eleven inches high — she felt unimportant
wonder who I was — they would be curious about her
proud of me — very pleased with me

EXERCISES

Exercise A: Recalling the Reading

Read each statement below and tell whether it is *true* or *false*. If the statement is false, correct it to make it a true statement.

1. Mary Antin came to the United States from Russia.
2. She admired George Washington because he was dead.
3. Mary Antin was Jewish.
4. Mary Antin discovered that she and George Washington were relatives.
5. Mary's poem made her father cry because he couldn't read English.
6. Mary's poem was published in the *Boston Transcript*.
7. Mary's poem was good because she had studied English for a long time.
8. Mary's father bought all the *Boston Heralds* he could find because he was proud of her.

Exercise B: Understanding the Reading

Summarize the main idea.

1. Quickly read the entire story again. In one sentence, tell your classmates why Mary Antin wrote the poem about George Washington.
2. Identify the person(s) or thing(s) referred to in each phrase. Pay special attention to the words in **boldface**.
    a. "**I** felt humble."
    b. "**He** never told a lie."
    c. ". . . **we** really had no country."
    d. ". . . **he** read it, tears came to **his** eyes . . ."
    e. "**She** said many kind things to me."
    f. "'Twas **he** who e'er will be our pride, . . ."
    g. "**He** stared at me and smiled."
    h. "**We** will print your poem."

i. **"They** would see my name . . ."

j. **"He** went out and bought all the *Boston Heralds* he could find."

Exercise C: Analyzing Ideas

Choose correct statements to complete the sentences below.

1. Mary Antin felt _____ because George Washington was a great man.
   - a. cheerful
   - b. depressed
   - c. brave
   - d. humble

2. Mary Antin believed that George Washington was her countryman because
   - a. he was a hero.
   - b. she was Jewish.
   - c. both of them were American citizens.

3. Mary Antin found her promised land
   - a. in Boston.
   - b. in Jerusalem.
   - c. in Russia.

4. Mary Antin wrote her poem because
   - a. Miss Dwight made her do it.
   - b. her father made her do it.
   - c. she discovered that George Washington was her fellow citizen.

5. Mary Antin read her poem to her classmates
   - a. because she looked heroic.
   - b. because it was a very long poem.
   - c. because it made her father cry.
   - d. none of the above.

6. The *Boston Transcript* didn't publish Mary's poem because
   - a. she was only eleven inches high.
   - b. Mary Antin was Jewish.
   - c. he didn't like the poem.
   - d. we don't know why.

7. Mary's father bought many copies of the *Boston Herald*
   a. because he had a lot of money.
   b. because he had a lot of friends.
   c. because he was proud of Mary.
   .d. because it was a Jewish holiday.

Exercise D: Word Study — Part I: Making Associations

Each of the following words is associated (connected) with one or more parts of the body or with the entire body.

tremble	twitch	shrug
embrace	stare	touch
point	bend	yell
cry	turn	knock

1. If you don't know some of these verbs, look them up in the dictionary, ask your teacher, or watch while someone performs the verb for you.

2. Which part or parts of the body do you use to perform these actions?

3. Notice that *all* of these verbs require subjects, but *not* all of the them require objects.

4. Act out one of the verbs for your classmates. Ask them to tell you which one it is.

Exercise D: Word Study — Part II: Meaning

Using the verb list from Part I, answer this question for *each* of the verbs:

1. Why would someone perform these actions: For example, *shrug* (shoulders). Why does someone do that? What does it mean when someone does it? A general answer would be: He or she doesn't know the answer to a question, so he or she shrugs.

2. There are many sensible reasons for the performance of these verbs. You will have your reasons and your classmates will have theirs. Watch and listen.

Exercise E: Questions for Discussion and Writing

1. How would you describe Mary Antin's idea of a *heroic* person? Do you agree with her description or not? Why?
2. Was Mary's discovery correct or not? Is Mary's discovery true today or not? Explain.
3. In paragraphs 4, 5, and 6 of Mary's story, she gives us her reasons for writing a poem. What are they? What do you think about them?
4. The main idea in "George Washington, My Countryman" is Mary's discovery of *equality* among Americans. Do you like this idea or not? Do you feel that *equality* is generally accepted in America or not? Explain.
5. George Washington's heroism is two hundred years old. Are there new heroes in America? Who are they? Why are they heroic?
6. Close your book and think about this story. Then write the answer to this question: Why is having a country to call her own so important to Mary Antin?

Exercise F: Additional Activity

Choose any modern hero in the last seventy-five years from any society that you know — your own society or another one. In a brief passage (a short composition), tell your reader these things:

- ❑ who this person is
- ❑ why you chose this person
- ❑ one great thing that this person has done
- ❑ why you think this action was heroic
- ❑ what has happened to this person

Please remember that heroes can be men or women; scholars, artists, or public figures (soldiers, politicians, doctors, etc.); young persons or adults of any color or race; dead or still living.

LESSON 11

Chinese School

The Writer

LAURENCE YEP (1948 –   )

Laurence Yep is a California writer; he was born in San Francisco in 1948. He holds a Ph.D. from the State University of New York at Buffalo.

He has written novels for young people and adults, and his work appears in several anthologies of science fiction.

The Reading

"Chinese School" is part of a larger work, a novel called *Child of the Owl*. The novel describes the life of a twelve-year-old girl named Casey. Casey's mother, who was a Chinese American, died when Casey was quite young, and Casey lived with her father for a time. When her father became too ill to look after her, Casey went to live with her grandmother. Casey's grandmother, whom everyone called Paw Paw, lived in San Francisco Chinatown. Paw Paw sent Casey to a Catholic  school so that Casey could learn English and Chinese, her mother's native language. For one hour each day, Casey had a special class in Chinese, taught by a Chinese teacher.

SHARING EXPERIENCES

Compare your responses with those of your classmates.

❏ How do teachers treat students in your country? Do they encourage students or make them feel stupid if they don't know the answer? In what ways are American teachers similar to or different from teachers in your country?

❏ Think about one of your teachers who was very strict. Did you like him or her? Did you respect him or her? Did you learn much from him or her?

❏ When you started studying English as a second language, could you understand your teachers? How did your teachers make you feel? Did they encourage you to try? Did you sometimes feel stupid?

❏ Is it difficult for you to write English words before you hear them? Why or why not? Do you sometimes memorize reading material before you know what it means?

❏ Do students from your culture who live in America take extra classes to learn their native language and culture? Why or why not?

As you read about this experience, notice the reasons for the conflict between Casey and the teacher. Notice the method of teaching that the teacher used. Casey's classmates seemed to learn Chinese, but Casey had problems.

Chinese School

Laurence Yep

The worst thing of all was Chinese school. I still get *nightmares* about it sometimes. I wasn't a bad student in the American school, but one hour out of each day the *nuns* left several classes and in would come the Chinese teachers. Right away they put me into the *dummies' class*, which met in an old room used to store old desks that were so old they had little holes with iron bottoms for putting ink bottles into. I found out quick enough that even this class was too *tough* for me. They taught school on the assumption that the kids already knew some Chinese, so they would explain the simple words in the textbooks with even simpler words — but I didn't even know those simple words.

2   The teacher was a plain-faced lady whose *pancake make-up* peeled in little patches so it looked like she had some kind of skin disease. She wore a sleeveless silk dress that *hugged her body* all the way down to her knees except for the slit that showed one leg.

---

nightmares — bad dreams
nuns — unmarried female Catholic teachers who devote their lives to God
dummies' class — (slang) — class for slow learners: "dumb students"
tough — (slang) — difficult
pancake makeup — liquid covered by powder
hugged her body — fit her body tightly

3   On Monday the teacher stood in front of the class to read that week's lesson from the thin little paperback that was our textbook. The lesson had a colored picture of ants crawling over a *rotten pomegranate* and the teacher explained the picture and story with a lot of hand gestures.

Then she started to read the story out loud again slowly, accenting each word carefully, and pausing after each sentence, which ended in an American-style period. Then she waved at the class to repeat the line. No one else was having trouble reading the words but all I saw was a bunch of *squiggly lines* so I took out my pencil to copy down the sounds I heard. I did that for about five sentences and then I heard the teacher. "What are you doing?" She spoke as if her mouth were full of *marbles* when she tried to speak English.

4   "I'm trying to write down the sounds." I held up my book. "See?"

5   The teacher's eyebrows came together and she *pursed her lips* as if she were having trouble *following* me and wording her own answer. "That no good. You . . . you think too much 'Merican. Not think Chinese. Never learn. You erase."

6   "But how am I going to be able to read the words out loud if I don't know what they sound like?"

7   I heard the teacher tap her foot impatiently. Even if she had enough English to explain — and I wasn't sure about that — she didn't want to take the time for just one dumb student. I didn't have to know Chinese to see that she ran her class like it was some well-oiled machine. She was so used to a *certain routine* that she hated to *break* it. "You erase," she insisted.

---

rotten pomegranate — spoiled red fruitfilled with seeds
squiggly lines — lines that go in several directions; Chinese writing
marbles — glass balls used by children for playing games
pursed her lips — put her lips together tightly
following — here, understanding
a certain routine — a way of doing things

8   "But how —"

9   "YOU ERASE." She snatched the book out of my hand and hit me with it. She didn't hit me hard enough to hurt, only to shock. Then she tossed my book back on top of my desk. "You *'Merican-born*. Lazy, Lazy, Lazy." Then she folded her left arm over her stomach and holding up her book in her right hand, she began to walk back up the aisle, reading the next sentence in the lesson. I sat for a while, listening to all the crazy sounds, and then I picked up my pencil and slowly began to erase what I had written, leaving the page without any meaning to me.

10   On Tuesday we had *calligraphy* where we'd insert a pattern of basic words inside sheets of *rice paper* and copy the words in ink — it was a bit like painting, so at first I liked it till the teacher slapped my wrist with a ruler for holding the brush wrong and then, because my wrist hurt, I did the words sloppy and got an F.

11   On Wednesday we got to recite the lesson from memory. The others had no trouble because they at least knew what sounds the words were supposed to be. I memorized as much of the lesson as I was able to get sounds for but even that made the teacher mad because while I think I got the sounds right, I didn't know the tones. Every word in Chinese has a tone — like when your voice rises at the end of a question. I just threw in a tone wherever I wanted, so that at first the teacher *winced* and finally just hid her face in the textbook and told me to sit down.

12   Thursday we copied the lesson out on narrow rectangles of rice paper that were *ruled off* in red ink into squares. You wrote a word in each square — which was pretty easy. But Friday we had to write the lesson out from memory. It was easier for the

---

break — here, change
'Merican-born — not native Chinese; born in America
calligraphy — writing that looks like drawing
rice paper — thin, fuzzy white paper
winced — looked as if she were in pain
ruled off — marked off by lines

other kids because it was a story to them, but to me the test meant I had to memorize a pattern of pictures. Still I did okay on that, getting every stroke in the right place. After I'd handed in my test, I sat back in my desk feeling pretty good. The teacher picked up her ballpoint pen and scanned over my test, frowning. Then she got up from her desk and came down the aisle. She clicked her pen shut and threw my test onto my desk. "How you do that? Not one word wrong."

13   "I learned the lesson," I said.

14   The teacher's lips moved silently, as if she were trying to figure out the words for what she wanted to say next. "This too good. You copy book when I not looking."

15   "I didn't copy any book," I said *indignantly*. "I don't cheat."

16   "You not speak Chinese. You not read. You not even hold brush right. And you do this?" Her voice rose angrily. "You copy book."

17   "I've got a good memory. Want to see me do it again?"

18   "You know not enough time. Only five minutes left. You copy book."

19   "Are you calling me a *liar*?" I was getting just as mad as she was.

20   She wanted to go into a real *tirade* then. The whole class had stopped whatever they were doing, turning to watch us. But she knew that if she did it in Chinese, I wouldn't understand her, so it would be wasted. And yet her English wasn't good enough or she was just too mad to think. All she could say was "You too dumb. You copy book." She said each sound like it was exploding from her mouth. Then she clicked her pen out and *stabbed my test paper* and *scrawled out a big F* across the surface. After that I just gave up trying.

---

indignantly — angrily
liar — someone who lies; doesn't tell the truth
tirade — fit of anger and shouting
stabbed my test paper — poked a hole in it
scrawled out a big F — wrote a big F for failure

21 The simplest thing would have been to go to Paw Paw and ask her to help me, but for one thing I never said I wanted to learn Chinese. I was an American and I couldn't see any good reason to learn a foreign language. And then, too, it *hurts your pride* when you think you're smart and you have to do things that make you feel dumb.

---

hurts your pride — makes you feel bad about yourself

EXERCISES

Exercise A: Recalling the Reading

Read each statement below and decide whether it is *true* or *false*. If the statement is false, correct it to make a true statement.

1. The narrator of "Chinese School" is a ten-year-old American boy.
2. The narrator knows basic Chinese vocabulary.
3. The narrator can't read Chinese writing.
4. The teacher doesn't want Casey to "write down sounds."
5. The teacher takes away Casey's book to punish her.
6. The teacher thinks that Casey is dumb and lazy.
7. Casey memorizes the lesson, but she can't use the right tones.
8. Casey thinks that she has done a good job of writing the lesson from memory.
9. The teacher accuses Casey of copying the book and then lying about it.
10. The teacher gives Casey an "F" for failure.
11. Casey quit Chinese school after a week of instruction.

Exercise B: Understanding the Reading

Summarize the main idea.

1. Quickly read the entire story again. In one sentence explain why the teacher gave Casey an "F" on her paper.
2. Identify the person(s) or thing(s) referred to in each phrase. Pay special attention to the words in **boldface**.
   a. "Right away **they** put me into the dummies' class, . . ."
   b. "**She** wore a sleeveless silk dress that hugged her body all the way down to her knees except for the slit that showed one leg."
   c. "Then **she** waved at the class to repeat the line."
   d. ". . . but all **I** saw was a bunch of squiggly lines so **I** took out my pencil to copy down the sounds **I** heard."

e. **"She** was so used to a certain routine that she hated to break it."

f. **"You** 'Merican born. Lazy, Lazy, Lazy."

g. ". . . because my wrist hurt, **I** did the words sloppy and got an F."

h. "It was easier for . . . because it was a story to them, . . ."

i. "All **she** could say was 'You too dumb.' "

j. ". . . it hurts **your** pride when **you** think you're smart and you have to do things that make you feel dumb."

Exercise C: Analyzing Ideas

Choose correct statements to complete the sentences below. You may have more than one answer for some sentences.

1. Casey has a basic problem in learning Chinese because
   a. she isn't very bright.
   b. the teacher doesn't speak clearly.
   c. Casey doesn't know simple Chinese words.

2. Casey copies what she hears the teacher read
   a. to write down the sounds.
   b. to teach herself Chinese writing.
   c. to make fun of the teacher.

3. The teacher dislikes Casey's way of remembering Chinese writing
   a. because the teacher has her own way of teaching.
   b. because Casey is lazy.
   c. because Casey doesn't try to learn.

4. The teacher dislikes Casey
   a. because Casey is Chinese.
   b. because Casey is American-born.
   c. because Casey is bigger than the teacher.

5. Casey succeeds in *writing* the lesson from memory
   a. because she learns the story.
   b. because she memorizes the "pictures" (Chinese characters).
   c. because she memorizes the tones of the words.

6. When the teacher accuses Casey of copying the book,
   a. Casey says that she has a good memory.
   b. Casey tells the teacher that the teacher's method is successful.
   c. Casey says that her success is just an accident.

7. Casey and the teacher of Chinese have a conflict
   a. because for English-speakers, Chinese is a very difficult language to speak and write.
   b. because the teacher and Casey have different ways of teaching and learning.
   c. because Casey really doesn't want to learn Chinese.

Exercise D: Word Study: Conditionals — *if, as if,* and *like*

1. In English we have ways of showing conditions that express uncertainty or that haven't happened yet. In Laurence Yep's story, you read sentences like these:
   i. "Even *if* she had enough English to explain . . ." (paragraph 7)
   ii. ". . . She pursed her lips *as if* she were having trouble following me . . ." (paragraph 5)
   iii. ". . . She ran her class *like* it was some well-oiled machine . . ." (paragraph 7)

2. In (i) and (ii), the narrator uses *if* and *as if* to express *uncertainty*. The teacher's knowledge of English is *unknown*, and the narrator uses *if* and *as if* to show doubt or uncertainty.

   In (iii), *like* is *informal speech*; it works the same way as *as if*.

3. Notice that *if* and *as if* are followed by *were* in (ii), where you would expect to see *was*. *Like* is followed by *was* because it is informal speech.

4. Try joining the sentences below using *if* and *as if*. You may change the order of the sentences if you need to do so. Change *was* to *were* whenever necessary.

Column A

1. I had a lot of money.
2. She treated me badly.
3. I wouldn't go to school at all.
4. I needed glasses.
5. The teacher slapped my hand.

Column B

a. I was stupid.
b. I would hire my own teacher.
c. I could go somewhere else.
d. I read slowly.
e. The teacher disliked me.

Exercise E: Questions for Discussion and Writing

1. Does Casey think the Chinese teacher is unattractive? How does she describe the teacher?
2. Does the Chinese teacher think that Casey is a troublesome student? How does the teacher behave toward Casey?
3. What do you think of the teacher's method of teaching Chinese?
4. Why does Casey have trouble learning Chinese?
5. Do you think that hitting or making fun of a student is a good way to teach? Discuss.
6. What should Casey have done during that first week of school?
7. Close your book and think about this reading. Write a response to this sentence:

   "I was an American and I couldn't see any good reason to learn a foreign language."

Exercise F: Additional Activity

Here is an incomplete dialogue between Casey and her grandmother, Paw Paw. Fill in the missing speech with a phrase or a sentence; write more if you like.

Casey comes home after school on the Friday afternoon she has failed her test.

Casey: Paw Paw, we need to talk.

Paw Paw: What's the matter, Casey? You look as if _____

_____ .

Casey: Look at this! (She shows Paw Paw her test.)
Paw Paw: _____ .
Casey: I know you don't understand, but I can't _____

_____ .

Paw Paw: Maybe the teacher isn't good. Suppose I help you?
Casey: Thank you, but _____ .
        If I wanted to learn _____

_____ .

Paw Paw: But your mother spoke Chinese before she learned
        English. Why _____ ?
Casey: Because I'm American. I don't need to _____

_____ .

        Anyway, I know I'm smart and I feel like _____

_____ .

Paw Paw: What_____ ?
Casey: I'm sorry, but I want to _____

_____ .

LESSON 12

Music Lady

The Writer

VICKIE L. SEARS

Vicki L. Sears is a writer, feminist therapist, and teacher living in Seattle, Washington. She says, "I have been writing since I was six." Her works have appeared in numerous publications.

The Reading

The narrator of "Music Lady" remembers herself as a nine-year-old Native American who wants to be a writer. We learn that the narrator's parents had died or disappeared, and the narrator lives in an orphanage. Sometimes the narrator escapes from the orphanage and runs all the way to a record store in the city. It is here that the narrator meets the "Music Lady," Mrs. Smith, who owns the record store and welcomes this young Native American to listen to music. Many years later, the narrator, now forty-five years old, returns to the music store, and Mrs. Smith is still there, as kind and helpful as ever.

There are references to music and musicians in "Music Lady." "Peter and the Wolf," by the Russian composer Prokofiev (ProKO-fee-eff) is a simple tale set to music and usually narrated by an actor. Billie Holiday was a famous African American singer of popular songs and "the blues." She died of drug abuse. Scott Joplin was an African American pianist and composer of a kind of popular music called "rag" or "ragtime." The reference to Beethoven (BAYtoven), the great German composer of the 19th century, expresses Beethoven's great emotions and the "storm scene" from his Pastoral Symphony. Haydn (HIEdon) was also a famous classical composer of the 18th century. In contrast to this music and these musicians, the narrator plays the music that her parents liked: Big Band music (Harry James, Woody Herman, Stan Kenton), her mother's favorite; and tribal (Native American) music, which she connects with her father.

SHARING EXPERIENCES

Compare your responses with those of your classmates.

1. What's your favorite kind of American music? Do you know any American recording artists? If so, who are your favorites?
2. What's your favorite record store? Are there other record or compact disk stores in your community? Why do you like this one better than the others? Are the salespeople helpful? Are there private listening booths?
3. When you were a child, was there a particular store that you liked to go to? Why?
4. Think about an adult (other than your parents) who encouraged you to develop a special talent. Who was that person? What did the person do to encourage you?

Music Lady

Vickie L. Sears

O n days of rain, when poetry often came to paper, I'd sneak away from the *orphanage*, running to leg tautness and chest burn all the way to 15th and 65th streets to the record store. That's where the music lady lived. Where there were sounds that made my poetry seem brighter. Where the music lady smiled under high cheekbones, patted my head, and whispered words of encouragement.

2   It wasn't an ordinary record store, then or now. It had listening *booths* and rows of deep wooden forest-green *troughs*

---

orphanage — a home for children without parents
booths — tiny rooms giving privacy for listening to music
troughs — containers; bins, like long boxes

filled with the faces of musicians and instruments. These were the instruments of the Big Band music my mother liked. Different from the flutes, bells, and drums of my father's family. Different, too, from the silence of the orphanage, except for the dinner bell. Here trumpets and cellos *blared in silence* from cardboard covers. Grownups strolled the aisles and *flicked* through the records, like playing cards, choosing their hand of music before taking it to one of the narrow rectangles, each equipped with *turntable* and speakers, to listen. The *sound-proofed booths* created individual worlds of *monophonic* magic seeping through the glass doors.

3   It never really mattered much what was playing, although I began to *gravitate* to jazz and playful Bach. Bach sounded of creek-skipping water and duck laughs. It was hard for me to understand how a man who dressed with lace edging his jacket and pants, and wearing such a *ponderous* wig, could have so much fun. Still, I'd walk beside the booths, *spiral binder* and pencil in hand, searching for just the right music to write near. As casually as a walnut-colored nine-year-old among the tall, mostly white adults could, I'd position myself against a booth's doorjamb and *lean an ear to sound*. I'd close my eyes for filling, follow the strings of music, and slip down into its colors. All other sounds faded. My body, rain rhythm, and the music became all. After awhile I could make a poem and slide back into the *downpour*, happy in its beat. I felt special in the rainsong and slow walk home.

4   One afternoon as I wandered the aisles, a slim creamed-skinned lady with *rouge-circled* cheeks motioned to me. As she *crooked her finger*, my first thought was to apologize for

---

blared in silence — they were photographs
flicked — moved their hands rapidly
turntable — a machine for playing records
sound-proofed booths — where other sounds were kept out
monophonic — melodic   **gravitate** — turn to
ponderous — large and heavy   **spiral binder** — notebook
lean an ear to sound — listen in from outside
downpour — heavy rain
rouge-circled — pink-colored circles of powder
crooked her finger — bent her finger, meaning "come here"

entering this secret world supposed to be for adults. Yet she didn't seem really threatening. Cautiously, I went toward the woman, noting the gray day through the window framing her pale *hazel* hair and the openness of her arms held still at either side of herself. She smelled of softness as she asked, "Would you like to have a booth for yourself?"

5   Magic!

6   The only thing I could say was, "I can't buy no music!"

7   A soft smile spread as she slowly shook her head asking, "No? Well, can you listen anyway?"

8   I jiggled an affirmative head. She said, "I'm Mrs. Smith, and this is my store so you're welcome here anytime."

9   Feeling drained away from my body as she took the tips of my fingers to lead me to a listening booth. There were no words as she bent toward me, asking, "Is there something special you'd like to hear?"

10   "No, Ma'am," *staggered out*, but Mrs. Smith, *undaunted* by my lacking, said, "Well, you wait here. I'll come back with something wonderful."

11   I wanted to run, but my legs weighed too heavy. An adult approached the booth, saying, "Oh, excuse me," just as though I belonged. I slid to the floor, sitting down as I *wrested* my folded spiral binder from my back pocket and my pencil from above my ear where writers always carried them. Mrs. Smith returned to my show of calm confidence and put on *Peter and the Wolf.* Story and music! How could she have known? Grownups usually didn't understand about such things. They often forgot their heart secrets. But the days that followed, where I could pick anything I wanted to listen to, proved me wrong. Billie Holiday sang sadness after I'd listen to tribal music and wonder where my father was. Big Band sounds signaled tears of missing mother, but Scott Joplin had a "Maple Leaf Rag" that warmed. Beethoven got mad and made thunderous rain. Haydn knew the calm of a sunny Lake Washington.

---

hazel — light brown   **staggered out** — here, said with difficulty
undaunted — not bothered   **wrested** — pulled out

12   Mrs. Smith asked what I was writing as though it were really important and not merely an adult being *tolerant*. She let me read her poem after poem without laughing or correcting the English or telling me not to dream. She'd say, "You keep doing that," and patted my head. I'd leave the music store with the feeling of being *cuddled* in sunlight, even in the rain. It was really quite all right to be a cross-eyed funny Indian kid who secretly scribbled poetry. Mrs. Smith said it was good. And all those different people of all those colors and looks on all those records knew it was too.

13   Many years later, when I was forty-five and *in a cold early-spring-drizzle mood*, I went into Standard Records and Hi-Fi feeling the need for some new music to match the time I wanted to spend writing. In one of the *floorworn* aisles still narrow with record bins, I stopped for the passage of an Elder. Her thin body, shoulder-stooped and year-wrinkled, slipped *sprightly* past me. She smiled at my having slightly bowed with hand gesturing for her to have right of way. A warm rush flooded over me. I watched her bending toward a customer, her *slight* hands softly bridging the width of a record as she placed it on a turntable. She had not been in the store the other times I had come since growing up. I waited until she was behind the counter again, then stood before her, feeling shy.

14   Mrs. Smith asked me if there was anything else I wanted other than the Billie Holiday I'd chosen. I *took in deep air* and said, "I want to thank you for all the times you listened to my poetry as a kid and for your patting my head."

15   A puzzled face turned up toward me, a broad smile *cresting her mouth*. I told her about her gift. She grinned more widely and said, "How nice that I could be there for you to save some beauty. The world needs people like you in it. Well, I'll pat your head again."

---

tolerant — agreeable; sympathetic   **cuddled** — held warmly
in a cold early-spring-drizzle mood — rainy and creative mood
floorworn — a well-used floor
sprightly — lightly and quickly   **slight** — small and slender
took in deep air — a big breath of air
cresting her mouth — parting her lips

EXERCISES

Exercise A: Recalling the Reading

Read each statement below and decide whether it is *true* or *false*. If the statement is false, correct it to make a true statement.

1. The narrator lives in an orphanage.
2. The narrator is a young Native American boy who writes music.
3. The narrator's parents liked music, too.
4. The narrator believes that listening to music helps her to write.
5. Mrs. Smith, the Music Lady, offers the narrator a booth where she can listen to music.
6. Mrs. Smith doesn't like the narrator's poetry.
7. When the narrator returns to the record store, she discovers that Mrs. Smith has died.

Exercise B: Understanding the Reading

Summarize the main idea

1. Quickly read the entire story again. In one sentence tell your classmates why the author liked to write her poetry while listening to music.
2. Identify the person(s) or thing(s) referred to in each phrase. Pay special attention to the words in **boldface**.
    a. "**Here** trumpets and cellos blared in silence from cardboard covers."
    b. ". . . created individual worlds of monophonic magic seeping through the glass doors."
    c. "It was hard for me to understand how a **man** who dressed with lace edging on his jacket and pants, and wearing such a ponderous wig, could have so much fun."
    d. "**I'd** close my eyes for filling, following the strings of music, and slip down into its colors."
    e. "**I'm** . . . and this is my store so you're welcome here anytime."

f. "... usually don't understand about such things."
g. "**Her** thin **body**, shoulder-stooped and year-wrinkled, slipped sprightly past me."
h. "A warm rush flooded over **me**."
i. "**I** told her about her gift."

Exercise C: Analyzing Ideas

Choose the best answers to complete the statements below.

1. The narrator escaped to the music store because _____

_____ .

2. The narrator's mother had liked _____ ,

but her father had liked _____ .

3. The narrator listened to music because she believed that

music _____ .

4. Mrs. Smith was kind to the narrator because _____

_____ .

5. Because of Mrs. Smith's kindness, the narrator returned to

the record store many years later, and _____

_____ .

Exercise D: Structure and Style: Figurative Language

Vickie Sears became a poet and prose-writer after the beginnings she described in "Music Lady." In this brief autobiographical piece, Ms. Sears uses "figures of speech" or "poetical language." Some examples of this language have been glossed for you already. Other examples were not explained.

In the left column below are examples of figurative or

"poetic" language. In the right column, write down an explanation that the figurative language suggests to you. Note: this ¶ is the symbol for paragraph. "¶8" means paragraph 8 of the reading.

Column A	Column B
1. ". . . running to leg tautness and and chest burn . . ."(¶1)	1.
2. ". . . deep wooden forest-green troughs filled with the faces of musicians . . ."(¶2)	2.
3. ". . . monophonic magic seeping through the glass doors." (¶2)	3.
4. ". . . a walnut-colored nine-year-old . . ." (¶3)	4.
5. "I jiggled an affirmative head. . . ." (¶8)	5.
6. "Big Band sounds signaled tears of missing mother . . ." (¶11)	6.
7. "Her thin body, shoulder-stooped and year-wrinkled . . ." (1¶3)	7.
8. ". . . her slight hands softly bridging the width of a record . . ." (¶13)	8.

Exercise E: Questions for Discussion and Writing

1. Why do you think the narrator is so shy when she first visits the record store?
2. How do music and poetry seem to work together for the narrator?
3. Why do you think that Mrs. Smith, the Music Lady, befriends the narrator, "a cross-eyed funny Indian kid who secretly scribbled poetry."?
4. Is there a special reason for the narrator to return to the record store thirty-six years later? Explain it.
5. How did Mrs. Smith's kindness help the shy kid to become a writer?

6. Close your book and think about the story. Explain why Mrs. Smith offered the use of a private listening booth in her record store to a nine-year-old Native American child who couldn't buy any music.

Exercise F: Additional Activities

1. Listen to different recordings of classical music (Bach, Beethoven, Haydn, Mozart). Try to identify the instruments (use the English words for them) playing different parts. Which recording do you like best? Why? Describe the sounds of the music on this recording.

2. Do you or any of your classmates listen to American jazz? Do you like it? Listen to the Big Band recordings brought to class. Describe the Big Band sound. Do you like it? Now listen to a recording by jazz singer Billie Holiday. How is her sound different from that of other American female vocalists you have heard? Finally, listen to Scott Joplin's "Maple Leaf Rag." Compare this sound to the Big Band sound. Which recording do you like better?

4

Ties

LESSON 13

I Know Why the Caged Bird Sings

The Writer

MAYA ANGELOU (1928 -   )

Maya Angelou, a native of Arkansas, is a celebrated African American poet, author, playwright, screenwriter, director, and civil rights leader. She has published five volumes of poetry, including the recently published volume *I Shall Not be Moved*. The book *I Know Why the Caged Bird Sings* is the first volume of a remarkable four-part autobiography. At the invitation of President William Clinton, Ms. Angelou composed and read a poem for his inaugural ceremony on January 20, 1993.

The Reading

This reading is from *I Know Why the Caged Bird Sings*. This book is about the childhood years that Maya Angelou and her older brother Bailey spent in the home of their paternal grandmother Henderson (whom the children called Momma) and Uncle Willie in the small rural town of Stamps, Arkansas.

SHARING EXPERIENCES

Compare your responses with those of your classmates.

❏ Have you lived in a small town? What was it like?

❏ Have you ever lived with relatives other than your parents? If so, whom did you live with? Is it unusual in your culture for children to live with relatives other than their parents? If so, why does this happen?

❏ Do you miss your parents when you live away from them? How do you feel when you receive gifts and letters from them?

I Know Why the Caged Bird Sings

Maya Angelou

People in Stamps used to say that the whites in our town were so *prejudiced* that a Negro couldn't buy vanilla ice cream. Except on July Fourth. Other days he had to be satisfied with chocolate.

---

prejudiced — here, anti-Negro

2   I couldn't understand whites and where they got the right to spend money so *lavishly*. Their wealth that allowed them to waste was the most *enviable*. They had so many clothes they were able to give perfectly good dresses, worn just under the arms, to the sewing class at our school for the larger girls to practice on.

3   Momma bought two *bolts* of cloth each year for winter and summer clothes. She made my school dresses, underslips, bloomers, handkerchiefs, Bailey's shirts, shorts, her aprons, house dresses and *waists* from the rolls shipped to Stamps by Sears and Roebuck. Uncle Willie was the only person in the family who wore ready-to-wear clothes all the time. Each day, he wore fresh white shirts and *flowered suspenders*, and his special shoes cost twenty dollars. I thought Uncle Willie sinfully *vain*, especially when I had to iron seven stiff starched shirts and not leave a *cat's face* anywhere. During the summer we went barefoot, except on Sunday, and we learned to *resole* our shoes when they "gave out," as Momma used to say.

4   The country had been in the Depression for two years before the Negroes in Stamps knew it. I think that everyone thought that the Depression, like everything else, was for the whitefolks, so it had nothing to do with them. Our people had lived off the land and *counted on* cotton-picking and hoeing and chopping seasons to bring in the cash needed to buy shoes, clothes, books and *light farm equipment*. It was when the owners of cotton fields dropped the payment of ten cents for a pound of cotton to eight, seven and finally five that the Negro

---

lavishly — spend so much money
enviable — desirable
bolts — rolls
waists — upper part of a dress; or a blouse
flowered suspenders — fancy-looking elastic to hold up trousers
vain — silly; foolish
cat's face — the mark left by a hot iron
resole — put new soles on our shoes
counted on — planned on
light farm equipment — tools for farm use

community realized that the Depression, at least, did not *discriminate*.

5   Welfare agencies gave food to the poor families, Black and white. Gallons of *lard*, flour, salt, powdered eggs and powdered milk. People stopped trying to raise hogs because it was too difficult to get *slop* rich enough to feed them, and no one had the money to buy mash or fish meal. We were among the few Negro families not *on relief*, but Bailey and I were the only children in the *town proper* that we knew who ate powdered eggs every day and drank the powdered milk. We were always given enough to eat, but we both hated the lumpy milk and mushy eggs, and sometimes we'd stop off at the house of one of the poorer families to get some peanut butter and crackers.

6   One Christmas we received gifts from our mother and father, who lived separately in a heaven called California, where we were told they could have all the oranges they could eat. And the sun shone all the time. I was sure that wasn't so. I couldn't believe that our mother would laugh and eat oranges in the sunshine without her children. Until that Christmas when we received the gifts I had been *confident* that they were both dead. I could cry anytime I wanted by picturing my mother (I didn't quite know what she looked like) lying in her coffin. Her hair, which was black, was spread out on a tiny little white pillow and her body was covered with a sheet. The face was brown, like a big O, and since I couldn't fill in the features I printed MOTHER across the O, and tears would fall down my cheeks like warm milk.

7   Then came that terrible Christmas with its awful presents. Our father sent his photograph. My gift from Mother was a tea

---

discriminate — choose among people
lard — animal fat for cooking
slop — remains of meals
on relief — receiving government help
town proper — within the city limits
confident — here, certain

set — a teapot, four cups and saucers and tiny spoons — and a doll with blue eyes and rosy cheeks and yellow hair painted on her head. I didn't know what Bailey received, but after I opened my boxes I went out to the backyard behind the chinaberry tree. The day was cold and the air was clear as water. Frost was still on the bench but I sat down and cried. I looked up and Bailey was coming from the *outhouse*, wiping his eyes. He had been crying too. I didn't know if he had also told himself they were dead and had been *rudely awakened* to the truth or whether he was just feeling lonely. The gifts opened the door to questions that neither of us wanted to ask. Why did they send us away? And what did we do so wrong? So Wrong? Why, at three and four, did we have tags put on our arms to be sent by train alone from Long Beach, California, to Stamps, Arkansas, with only the *porter* to look after us? (Besides, he got off in Arizona.)

8   Bailey sat down beside me, and that time didn't *admonish* me not to cry. So I wept and he sniffed a little, but we didn't talk until Momma called us back in the house.

9   Momma stood in front of the tree that we had decorated with silver ropes and pretty colored balls and said, "You children *is* the most *ungrateful things* I ever did see. You think your momma and poppa went to all the trouble to send you these nice play pretties to make you go out in the cold and cry?"

10   Neither of us said a word. Momma continued, "Sister, I know you tender-hearted, but Bailey Junior, there's no reason for you to set out mewing like a pussy cat, just 'cause you got something from Vivian and Big Bailey." When we still didn't force ourselves to answer, she asked, "You want me to tell

---

outhouse — toilet
rudely awakened — shocked into believing
porter — a worker who handles baggage on a train
admonish — warn
is — (dialect) are
ungrateful things — (dialect) people who don't feel thankful for good things they receive

Santa Claus to take these things back?" A wretched feeling of being torn *engulfed* me. I wanted to scream, "Yes. Tell him to take them back." But I didn't move.

11   Later Bailey and I talked. He said if the things really did come from Mother maybe it meant that she was getting ready to come and get us. Maybe she had just been angry at something we had done, but was *forgiving* us and would send for us soon. Bailey and I tore the stuffing out of the doll the day after Christmas, but he warned me that I had to keep the tea set in good condition because any day or night she might come riding up.

---

engulfed — flowed over; covered
forgiving — excusing; pardoning

EXERCISES

Exercise A: Recalling the Reading

Read each statement below and decide whether it is *true* or *false*. If the statement is false, correct it to make a true statement.

1. Maya Angelou grew up in Alabama.
2. She lived with her grandparents and her Uncle Willie.
3. The Depression took place in the 1940s.
4. African Americans worked the farms of white people who owned the land.
5. Welfare agencies gave food to poor families during the Depression.
6. Maya and Bailey loved the food provided by the welfare agencies.
7. Maya believed that both of her parents were dead.
8. Maya and Bailey cried because they disliked their parents.
9. Maya's grandmother threatened to send the gifts back.
10. Maya and Bailey thought they had been sent away because they did something wrong.

Exercise B: Understanding the Reading

Summarize the main idea.

1. Quickly read the entire story again. In one sentence, tell your classmates why Maya and Bailey cried when they received Christmas gifts.
2. Identify the person(s) or thing(s) referred to in each phrase. Pay special attention to the words in **boldface**
   a. "Other days **he** had to be satisfied with chocolate."
   b. ". . . **they** were able to give perfectly good dresses, worn just under the arms, to the sewing class at our school . . ."
   c. ". . . was the **only person** in the family who wore ready-to-wear clothes all the time."
   d. "During the summer **we** went barefoot . . ."

e. "... **everyone** thought that the Depression, like everything else, was for whitefolks, so it had nothing to do
with them."

f. "**We** were always given enough to eat ..."

g. "**Her** hair, which was black, was spread out on a tiny little
white pillow and her body was covered with a sheet."

h. "I didn't know if **he** had also told himself they were dead
and had been rudely awakened to the truth or whether
he was just feeling lonely."

i. "**You** think your momma and poppa went to all the
trouble to send you these nice play pretties to make you
go out in the cold and cry?"

j. "A wretched feeling of being torn engulfed **me**."

Exercise C: Analyzing Ideas

Choose correct statements to complete the sentences below.

1. Whitefolks were able to spend money so lavishly because
   a. the Depression didn't matter to them.
   b. they had more money to spend.
   c. they were lazy.

2. The Depression came to Stamps, Arkansas
   a. because the whitefolks spent all their money.
   b. when the government took away people's tools.
   c. when the price of cotton dropped from ten cents to five
      cents a pound.

3. The Depression didn't discriminate between African
   Americans and whitefolks because
   a. America was a democracy.
   b. everyone stopped working.
   c. rich slop wasn't available.

4. Maya and Bailey hated the food from welfare agencies
   because
   a. it tasted unpleasant.
   b. it was free.
   c. whitefolks made African Americans eat it.

5. Maya believed that her parents were dead because
   a. she hadn't heard from them.
   b. her grandmother told her they were dead.
   c. they lived in a place called Atlanta and ate oranges.

6. Maya and Bailey thought that they were sent to Arkansas
   a. because they did something wrong.
   b. because their grandmother needed their help on the farm.
   c. because of the great Depression.

Exercise D: Connectives and Compound Sentences

1. The words *but* and *so* are used often in speech and writing to connect sentences. These two words have different *meanings*. Where they join sentences, *but* suggests opposition or a kind of negation: A *but* (not) B. *So* suggests a result, a consequence: C (and) *so* (therefore) D.

2. Some of the sentences below can be (1) joined by *but*; (2) joined by *so*: (3) joined by both *but* and *so*. You can join sentences from column A to Column B and from Column B to Column A. When you join sentences using both *but* and *so*, be sure that you can explain the differences in meaning.

Column A	Column B
1. I wanted a different present	a. I couldn't tell people how I felt
2. I was angry at him	b. I left the park early
3. I thought that he was foolish	c. some people disagreed with me
4. I tried to be amusing	d. she wouldn't speak to me
5. I didn't think she was interesting	e. he didn't leave
6. He was sick and tired and wanted to go home	f. I didn't enjoy my dinner
7. I thought that the food tasted wonderful	g. nobody seemed to care

Example: ___ I was angry at him, but I couldn't ___

___ tell people how I felt. ___

Exercise E: Questions for Discussion and Writing

1. What was the biggest difference between whites and African Americans in Stamps, Arkansas?
2. When the price of cotton dropped, what did the African American community finally understand?
3. How did the Great Depression affect both whites and African Americans in Stamps?
4. Why did Maya and Bailey think that their parents were dead?
5. Why was Christmas "terrible" and why were the presents "awful"?
6. Why did Maya and Bailey think their parents had sent them away?
7. Why did Maya have a "feeling of being torn"?
8. What might happen "any day or night"? How should Maya and Bailey prepare?
9. Why did Maya and Bailey go outside and cry after opening the gifts? What did Bailey say about the gifts? Why did the children tear the stuffing out of the doll the day after Christmas?

LESSON 14

The Red Dog

The Writer

HOWARD MAIER

Howard Maier first published "The Red Dog" in 1950. Since then, this story has been published in several short-story collections.

The Reading

There is an old saying in English: "A dog is man's best friend." We may also ask, "Is man a dog's best friend?" "The Red Dog" is a story that asks that question.

SHARING EXPERIENCES

Compare your responses with those of your classmates.

❏ What kinds of pets are kept by people in your native country? What kinds of pets have you had? How did you feel about your pets?

❏ What do you know about Americans and their pets? Do you think they are too attached to their pets? Why or why not? Give examples from media and personal observations of how Americans regard their pets.

❏ Have you ever lost a pet? How did you feel about the loss or death of your pet?

The Red Dog

Howard Maier

T his is the story of a dog. An Irish setter named Spook. In him *flowed* the blood of an *ancient line*; his *regality* was evident in the grace with which he carried himself, in the lift of his head,

---

flowed — ran (used for liquids like water and blood)
ancient — very old breed of dogs
regality — royalty

the dignity of his step, and his deep red *mahogany* coat. From the tip of his sensitive nose to the feathery sword of his tail, he was a king — a king who ruled me with the gentle power of love.

2   When the war came, Spook was my most serious problem. The Army would take care of me, but who would take care of Spook? For weeks I *wrestled with* the problem and could find no solution. In desperation — for it was almost time to go — I put the setter in the car and drove to a little town upstate where I had spent my summers. The owner of a local garage was an old friend of mine with whom I had often hunted.

3   Would he take Spook? *No strings attached*? (The war had just begun and who had the courage to *forecast* his own return from it?) But would he *hunt him*? Would he take good care of him? And most important of all and impossible to put into words, would he love him? I was giving him my dog — and with dogs you cannot give and take back.

4   Yes, my friend said, he would take him and hunt him and care for him. But he said nothing about love; for though men may write this word, they rarely use it. I watched him as he patted the dog's head and the hand was gentle, and Spook thumped the floor with his tail, but his eyes remained fixed on my face.

5   All the way up in the car he had watched me instead of hanging himself half out of the window in his customary manner; a dog senses many things besides game. Without another word, I handed my friend the *lead* and got into my car and drove away; and even today I cannot truly remember whether I heard Spook bark or I only imagined it. Generally I

---

mahogany — red-brown color
wrestled with — struggled with; fought with
no strings attached — without asking for something in return
forecast — tell the future
hunt him — use him as a hunting dog
lead — British English for leash - a leather strap or chain to restrain a dog while walking

am a slow and careful driver; but that day I drove for ten miles at top speed before slowing down.

6   After a month in the Army I wrote my friend a letter inquiring after the dog. I received no reply. Each camp was *farther afield*, and from each camp I wrote a letter. No answer ever came. I began to write to other friends in the village; and in each letter I asked for news of my dog. Some of them answered — but of those that did, none spoke of the dog. Spook is dead, I thought. He must be — otherwise they would answer. Rather than *face the actuality* of it, I gave up making inquiries and tried my best to put the dog from my mind.

7   Four years passed; the war was over; I had married and my wife and I lived in the city. Summer was here and we had taken a small house in the upstate village for our vacation. As we packed the bags in the car, Laurette suddenly looked up and said, "Suppose we run into your Spook?"

"Spook is dead," I said; she took one look at my face and never finished her question.

The minute we arrived at the village I drove to the garage although the tank was still half full. I left Laurette in the car and went into the office. My friend greeted me as if only a weekend had intervened since our last meeting, as if there had been no war, as if there had never been a question of a dog between us. Finally I couldn't stand it any longer and *blurted out*, "What happened to Spook?"

8   "Why nothing happened to him," my friend said. "He's as *hale and hearty* as you or I. I saw him only the other day."

My relief was so sharp that there was no room for anger. Bewildered, I asked, "What do you mean you saw him? Don't you have him anymore?"

9   At that he had the grace to look *shamefaced*. He said, "I was

---

farther afield — farther from home
face the actuality — accept the truth
blurted out — spoke loudly and quickly
hale and hearty — very healthy
shamefaced — ashamed

drafted, and I didn't know I was going to be turned down, so I gave him away to a minister, lives up above Willow."

"Why didn't you answer my letter?"

His face flushed with embarrassment. *"I'm no hand at writing,"* he said. "Don't think I've written a letter in ten years."

I stared at him. Was it possible that he, having read my letters pleading for news of the dog, didn't realize what Spook meant to me?

10 The fact that he didn't was written on his honest, embarrassed face. He was *country-bred*. To him a dog was an animal; it slept outdoors with the other animals and when fall came it was hunted, and that was all.

"What's the name of the minister?" I asked him.

"Oh, Spook's not with him anymore. To tell the truth, he's had five, maybe six masters since then. Lives up with some summer people named Crocker now, up past Shady. He's a valley dog now."

"A valley dog?"

11 "On his own. *Cruises* back and forth. Twenty miles one way or the other's nothing to him. Perfect condition, hard as nails. In the fall a man goes out with a gun and there's Spook ready and willing to tag along."

There was nothing to say; it was obvious that he thought the life of a valley dog the best possible life any dog could have.

"Sorry about the letter," he said, still ashamed.

12 "It's alright." I paid for my gas and went out to the car. I drove the mile to the house without saying anything. All the way Laurette kept looking at me. When we turned into the drive, she said gently, "Spook's alive, isn't he?"

13 I nodded my head and we let it go at that. After dinner I told her the whole story and she let me tell it without asking

---

I'm no hand at writing — I'm no good at writing. (I don't write well.)
country-bred — without much education
cruises — moves from one place to another , for pleasure

any questions. At the end, she asked, "Are you going to try to see him?"

"Well, sure," I said. "Why not?"

"I wouldn't," Laurette said. "It would only hurt you, and it would hurt him more. Don't try to find him; it sounds as if he's very happy now."

"Don't be silly. Do you think he'd remember me? After four years and six masters?"

14 She just looked at me and that was the end of the discussion. Two weeks passed and we worked and went swimming and lay around and we never talked about the dog.

Then one day I saw Spook.

15 During a climb up the side of the valley I had stopped to rest on a rock which overlooked an open pasture in the woods beneath us. A boy of about sixteen came out of the trees, and then a second later Spook raced out into the sunlight. I knew him at once. I would have known Spook anywhere.

16 The boy walked straight across the pasture; but Spook, as was his habit, *quartered the field*, racing far ahead, then back again. And all the time the sun was *glancing* from his coat as if from a shield of *burnished* copper. I had seldom seen him look so well or so beautiful. It took them about three minutes to cross the field; then the *trees on the far side swallowed* them both. The pasture had never been so empty.

17 When I returned to the house I told Laurette about it. She said, "Away up there on the side of the hill — how could you know it was Spook?"

"How do I know you're you?"

18 The next time I saw Spook, Laurette was with me. It was night, during one of those heavy summer rainstorms that

---

quartered the field — ran through two sections (quarter), looking for animals to hunt
glancing — shining
burnished — polished
trees on the far side swallowed — the boy and the dog disappeared from view

come up so suddenly. We were having dinner on the covered terrace of the local restaurant. *Padding* up the street came a dog, head down, tail down, looking as miserable as only an Irish setter can when it's soaking wet. As the dog came into the light cast by the terrace lamps, I said, "That looks like Spook." I must have pronounced the name quite loudly, for the dog stopped and his head came up. It was Spook.

19   He pushed in the screen door, walked across the *flagged* terrace, water dripping form his matted coat, and came up to my side. He stood there looking into my face for a minute, then — without a bark or a wag of his tail — curled up on the stone at my feet. He dropped his head on his paws, but never once closed his eyes; he watched every move I made, just the way he used to. Four years, four long years, I thought, and felt all sort of *choked up*. The waitress brought our food; at the sight of the wet dog, she said, "Here you . . ."

"Let him be!" I said, so sharply that the woman was startled. Laurette explained to her. Once during the meal I got up to go into the main dining room. Spook got up and went with me, all the way there and back, his head so close to my leg that my trousers brushed against him.

20   When we left the restaurant, Spook followed us; when I opened the door of the car, he was first in, over the front seat, and into his accustomed place in the right-hand back corner, his head pressed against the window.

21   "What are you going to do?' Laurette asked me.

"What can I do on a night like this?" I asked. She nodded her head understandingly.

"Let's go home, then."

We took Spook back to the little house with us. The open fire dried out his coat and the *feathers* on his legs and tail got all

---

padding — walking on paws (or walking softly)
flagged — stone; flagstone
choked up — very sad; near tears
feathers — long hair

curly and blonde. He lay there on the floor between Laurette's chair and my desk, his head toward me. If I stood up, he was instantly on his feet. At about ten o'clock, exactly as he had always done, he came over to my chair, placed a paw on my knee, cocked his head to one side and gazed silently into my face.

"What does he want?" Laurette asked.

22   "Out," I said, and I got up and opened the screen door for him. The rain had stopped and the moon had risen. Staring out into the darkness which had swallowed up the dog, I said over my shoulder, "Well, that's that, I guess. He'll go home now, to wherever home is." And for an instant I was filled with regret that I had so sternly held myself back from touching him or even so much as speaking to him in the old, intimate way.

23   Back at the desk I couldn't work. I stared at the blank paper in my typewriter. The paper didn't even exist for me, nor the room — not even Laurette existed for me. I was caught in the world outside the house: *my ears strained* for the slightest whisper or rustle in the grass.

24   At about eleven, two quick, *imperious* barks sounded outside the screen door. Laurette lifted her eyebrows inquiringly.

"He wants in," I told her. I jumped up from my chair and stood there helplessly in the center of the room, not knowing what to do.

"Well, go on, let him in," she said. "We'll talk later."

25   So I let him in, and when we went to bed he took his usual position on the floor beside my bed. I could hear him there, breathing softly in the darkness. Laurette talked to me.

"This is why I didn't want you to see him again," she said.

26   "But he was only two years old when I left him, and after four years, who would believe he's remembered me this way?" His act of remembrance had been with me all night. It was a wonderful thing.

---

my ears strained — I listened very carefully
imperious — commanding

"It's just as if I had never gone away," I said.

27 "Try not to think of that," Laurette said. "Think of Spook. Think how beautiful and fit he is, and remember that he's leading the proper life for a dog. A whole valley to roam in. What kind of life would he lead with us in the big city? With both of us working, what could he have? A walk on a lead twice a day? Never any grass, or any sun — never to run free. You wouldn't want to take him back to that, now that he's had the other, would you?"

"But I'm not doing anything," I protested. "I haven't even petted him. He's doing it all himself."

"The decision is up to you. You have to make it."

"All right, then," I said. "We'll take him back to the Crockers tomorrow."

28 She reached across and patted my arm and said no more. I don't know how long it took me to get to sleep that night. All I remember now is that once during the night I heard Spook get up and change position; I heard him hit the floor with a thud the way setters do. As he stretched out again I heard him sigh, a sound that seemed to contain all the contentment in the world.

29 We started for the Crockers' place at noon the next day. It was blazing hot. We drove the five miles in complete silence, except for Spook, who occasionally would whine anxiously deep in his throat.

30 We turned off the road and up the lane and circled the drive of the big house. When I took Spook out of the car, my fingers were tight about his collar; he was whining continually, and nothing in the world could have made me look into his eyes.

31 The boy I had seen in the pasture that other morning answered my knock; he looked *astounded* at seeing me with the dog. And all the time I talked to him, explaining what had happened, Spook kept pulling to break my hold on his collar.

---

astounded — very surprised

At last the boy understood the situation and took hold of Spook's collar, and I got back in the car and drove off.

32 We had gone only about a mile on the *macadam* when I saw him in the rear-view mirror. He was racing after the car, *running his heart out.*

33 "That fool kid let him loose!" I said, and put on the speed, but I couldn't tear my eyes from the mirror. He kept running and running, and the sun kept beating down on him, and I knew he would never give up. Suddenly Laurette said in a tense voice, "Do you want to kill him? Stop the car. Stop the car, do you hear?"

34 Pulling off the road and onto the grass, I got out of the car and waited. Spook came up and sank exhausted at my feet, his chest *laboring painfully*, his tongue hanging from his mouth. There was a little sound from the car and I turned around. Laurette was crying softly, the tears running down her cheeks.

35 "Spook, poor Spook," she kept saying through her sobs. "Don't worry anymore, not anymore please. We'll take him with us. It'll be all right, fine. You can walk him in the morning before you go to work, and I'll come home on my lunch hour and take him then. And Bessy won't mind taking him out once in the afternoon." Bessy was our maid. "We'll manage somehow," Laurette said.

36 I patted her shoulder and gave her my handkerchief. I put Spook back in the car and turned it around and headed back for the Crocker place. Laurette put a *restraining hand on my arm.*

"No, dear," I said. "It wouldn't work. Last night you *talked with your head*; now you're *talking with your heart*. Believe me, the head's better."

---

macadam — road made with layers of asphalt and small broken stones; named after the Scottish engineer, John McAdam.
running his heart out — killing himself by running too fast
laboring painfully — breathing with great difficulty
a restraining hand on my arm — an attempt to stop him
talked with your head — spoke reasonably
talking with your heart — speaking emotionally

37 This time I told the boy to lock Spook in the house and when we drove away, I drove very fast and Laurette said nothing about the speed.

38 All this took place more than three years ago. Today I rarely think of Spook, consciously anyway. But three or four times every year, I have *a recurring dream*, a horrible nightmare.

39 The scene of the dream is always the same; at the stretch of macadam highway. I am myself, in the car, and at the same time I am Spook — and I run and run and the car never stops, and the hard, cruel road hits my paws and the sun beats down on me and I keep saying over and over again: He doesn't want me, he doesn't want me. And then I feel a grief so sharp that I cannot contain it, and my heart swells and swells and *threatens to burst* with the sheer pity of it. At this point I always wake up in a cold sweat and I slip quietly out of the bed, for I have never told Laurette about the recurring dream.

40 I go into the living room and light a cigarette and stare out of the window. The streets are empty; the dark, cold stone houses *hem them in*. There are no trees, and that helps. I force myself to remember Spook as I saw him that day in the green pasture running free, with the soft grass beneath his feet and the wind whipping his ears back and the sun striking from his gleaming copper coat. That helps, too.

41 I put out my cigarette and go back to bed and to sleep. But even now, three years later, even now after writing it all down, I do not know whether the decision I made for Spook was right or wrong.

---

a recurring dream — the same dream again and again
threatens to burst — is ready to explode
hem them in — surround them

EXERCISES

Exercise A: Recalling the Reading

Read each statement below and decide whether it is *true* or *false*. If the statement is false, correct it to make a true statement.

1. Spook was a German shepherd.
2. The author and his wife lived in the country.
3. This story was written after a war.
4. The author worried about Spook while he was in the army.
5. Spook had just two owners: the author and the garage owner.
6. The author was away from Spook for four years before he saw the dog again.
7. Spook looked healthy and beautiful after four years of country life.
8. Spook didn't remember his old master when the two met after four years.
9. The author didn't take Spook to the city to live because he didn't think Spook would be happy there.
10. The author is sure that he made the right decision for Spook by leaving him in the country.

Exercise B: Understanding the Reading

Summarize the main idea.

1. Quickly read the entire story again. In one sentence explain to your classmates why the author took Spook back to the Crockers' house to live.
2. Identify the person(s) or thing(s) referred to in each phrase. Pay special attention to the words in **boldface**.
   a. "From the tip of **his** sensitive nose to the feathery sword of **his** tail, **he** was a king . . ."
   b. "For weeks **I** wrestled with the problems and could find no solution."
   c. "And most important of all and impossible to put into words, would **he** love him?"

d. "**I** began to write to other friends in the village; and in each letter **I** asked for news . . ."

e. "**He** was country-bred. To **him** a dog was an animal . . . and that was all."

f. "After dinner I told her the whole story and **she** let me tell it without asking any questions."

g. "I had seldom seen **him** look so well or so beautiful."

h. "**He** stood there looking into my face for a minute, then —without a bark or wag of **his** tail — curled up on the stone at my feet."

i. "**His** act of remembrance had been with me all night."

j. ". . . **he** looked astounded at seeing me with the dog."

k. "Do **you** want to kill him? . . ."

l. "Last night **you** talked with your head; now **you're** talking with your heart."

m. "But three or four times every year, **I** have a recurring dream, a horrible nightmare."

Exercise C: Analyzing Ideas

Choose correct statements to complete the sentences below.

1. The author of this story is probably a
   a. mechanic.   b. doctor.   c. professional writer.

2. Since this story was published in 1950, the war referred to in the story was probably
   a. World War I.   c. The Vietnam war.
   b. World War II.

3. Spook was a _____ dog.
   a. regal looking   b. clumsy looking   c. small

4. The author had to leave Spook with someone else
   a. when he got married.
   b. when he went into the army.
   c. when Spook grew unhappy living in the city.

5. The author had no news of Spook for four years because
  a. he had no one to write to in the village.
  b. his friends in the village didn't answer his questions about Spook.
  c. his wife didn't know where Spook was.

6. When the author went to the village with his wife for a vacation,
  a. he was thinking about Spook.
  b. he had forgotten about Spook.
  c. he didn't ask about Spook for a long time.

7. The garage owner
  a. felt the same way about Spook as the author did.
  b. understood the author's concern about his dog.
  c. didn't understand how the author felt about his dog.

8. When Spook came into the restaurant one rainy night,
  a. he was thrown out by the waitress.
  b. he recognized his old master and went to his side.
  c. he reacted to his old master as if he were a stranger.

9. On the rainy night that Spook and his old master were reunited, it was obvious
  a. that the dog and his master were glad to be with each other.
  b. that the author's wife, Laurette, didn't care for Spook.
  c. that Spook and his master were no longer friends.

10. The decision to leave Spook behind in the country village was _____ for the author.
  a. tiresome   b. easy   c. difficult

Exercise D: Descriptive Words

Howard Maier, the author of "The Red Dog," wants us to see and know Spook. Maier describes his appearance and his behavior.

Look through the story again and see which descriptive words and phrases answer these questions:
  i. What *color* is Spook?
  ii. How does he *move*?
  iii. How does he *behave* towards his master?

Write down the words that *show* you this dog. You can change word forms if you like — *watched* can be *watchful*; *regality* can be *regal*.

Exercise E: Combining Sentences with Verb + *ing*

When the subject of two sentences is the same, the sentence can often be combined into a single sentence by using a participial phrase (verb + *-ing*) to modify the subject.

Examples: a. John was sitting on the steps. He looked old and tired.
Sitting on the steps, John looked old and tired.

b. I pulled off the road. I got out and waited for Spook.
Pulling off the road, I got out and waited for Spook.

Directions: Combine the pairs of sentences below into single sentences with participial phrases. Decide whether the first or second sentence should be used as the Verb + *-ing* phrase.

1. He looked in the window. He saw a dog.

    _____

2. She waited for a bus. She ran into an old friend.

    _____

3. The dog appeared healthy. The dog padded into the restaurant.

    _____

4. He left the supermarket. Tom glanced at the garage across the street.

    _____

5. He looked at the dog. He felt very sad.

    _____

6. He glanced in the rear-view mirror. He saw Spook running his heart out.

    _____

7. I heard a sound from the car. I turned around.

    _____

8. I talked to him. I explained what happened.

    _____

9. I patted her shoulder. I gave her my handkerchief.

_____

10. I wake up in a cold sweat. I slip quietly out of bed.

_____

Exercise F: Questions for Discussion and Writing

1. Explain the problem or conflict in the story in your own words.
   a. What kind of feeling did the author have for Spook?
   b. How did Spook seem to feel about his master?
   c. Is the life of a valley dog better for Spook than living in the big city with the author?

2. Do you think that people should allow themselves to become very attached to animals so that they treat them almost like humans? Explain your answer.

3. What do you think of the author's decision to leave Spook in the village?
   a. Did he do the right thing for the dog?
   b. Give reasons to support your answer.

4. Why does the author have nightmares?
   a. When he dreams that he is Spook, how does he feel about his master?
   b. How does the author prefer to remember Spook?

Exercise G: Additional Activity

Write a two-paragraph composition with the title "Remembering the Red Dog."

In the first paragraph, complete this opening clause: "When I think about Spook, I remember most of all . . ." Then continue and tell the other qualities of Spook's appearance and behavior that you remember.

In the second paragraph, complete this opening dependent clause: "After the author found Spook again, I . . ." Then continue and tell those events in the story that made you feel as you did when you finished reading "The Red Dog."

LESSON 15

SURVIVOR

The Writer

JOHN DENNIS (1920 –)

John Dennis was born in 1920 in San Jose, California. He recently retired from teaching after a career of fifty years. Professor Dennis wrote "Survivor" after spending an afternoon talking with two young Vietnamese men, whose stories of escape were combined. The narrator, Thi Nham Binh, and the setting were also taken from real life. John Dennis has won numerous awards as a teacher and developer of programs in English as a Second/Foreign Language. He has published widely. "Survivor" and "George Washington, My Country-man" appeared in his textbook, *O, Promised Land*. Professor Dennis is one of the authors of *Reflections*.

The Reading

This is a narrative about the war in Vietnam told by a young woman who survived the destruction of Saigon; the destruction of her family; a shipwreck; abuse and humiliation by a relative; and constant loneliness living in the United States.

You may remember Solzhenitsyn's fable, "The Bonfire and the Ants" as you read "Survivor." What is the connection between the two?

SHARING EXPERIENCES

Compare your responses with those of your classmates.

❏ Share what you know about Vietnamese refugees in America. Why did they have to leave their homeland? What were the conditions of their escape? Where were the refugee camps in which they waited to come to America? Why were so many brought to the United States as refugees?

❏ Are you or any of your classmates refugees or immigrants from another country? If so, how is your life now different from the life you had in your native country? Was there a war going on in your country when you left? If it is not too difficult for you to talk about it, tell your classmates about your departure from your country.

❏ If you are studying English outside your native country, do you feel that you are among strangers? Why or why not?

❏ What do you do when you feel very lonely? How do you feel when professionals such as teachers, counselors, or caseworkers try to help you?

Survivor (Part I)

John Dennis

The woman who answers the door is short, gray-haired and middle-aged. She is drying her hands on her *apron*.

2 "Yes?" she says, looking at the two women standing in the doorway.

---

apron — a cloth worn to protect clothing

3   The older woman says, "I'm Miss Green from The Skills Center and this is Mrs. Nguyen. . . . You called about Miss Binh."

4   "Oh yes. Come in." She stands aside as the two women enter the hallway of the *rooming house*. "I'm Mrs. Kincaid, and . . ." she pauses.

5   "Yes?" says Miss Green.

6   "Well," Mrs. Kincaid continues, "I'm worried about Miss Binh. She hasn't left her room for two days. . . . Now I don't make a practice of *snooping* but I have gone to Miss Binh's room on *two occasions*. The door is locked, and I heard the sounds of someone crying. I thought I should tell you."

7   "Yes, thank you. We'll go up. Which apartment is she in?"

8   "Number 204 on the second floor. . . . Poor little thing. I hope she's all right." She watches them climb the stairs.

9   Mrs. Nguyen speaks to Thi Nham Binh through the door. She uses their native language. Miss Binh's voice sounds small and very far away. "Please open the door, Thi Nham," says Mrs. Nguyen. "We have come to help you."

10   After a short time, there is a soft clicking sound. Mrs. Nguyen nods to Miss Green. Miss Green says, "You do the talking. I'll listen, and maybe I'll have some questions. Okay?"

11   The room that they enter is filled with sunlight from four large windows. Thi Nham Binh sits in a chair at a table. She is dressed in American blue jeans and a white blouse with long sleeves, and she is *barefoot*. She is looking out the window onto the street below.

12   Mrs. Nguyen greets her cheerfully. Thi Nham Binh turns and stares at her visitors. She does not smile. She gets up slowly and bows slightly to Miss Green. She points to two chairs, and her visitors sit down. Thi Nham Binh turns away,

---

rooming house — a house with rooms for rent
snooping — watching other people
two occasions — twice
barefoot — without shoes or stockings

sits down and continues to stare at the street below. "Shall we speak in English?" Mrs. Nguyen asks. "Miss Green won't understand Vietnamese." This Nham Binh shrugs her shoulders. "We can try," she replies. She has been studying English in America for the past year and a half. She speaks French and *Cantonese* fluently.

13 "You have been absent from school and from work for the past two days. Your *landlady* telephoned us. You are not well?"

14 Thi Nham Binh does not reply.

15 "You require medical attention?"

16 Thi Nham Binh shakes her head.

17 "No?"

18 "No," say Thi Nham Binh. "There is no medicine for my illness."

19 "What is it, then?" Miss Green asks.

20 "A broken heart," says Thi Nham Binh. "I would like to return to Saigon. I know it is hopeless. My mother is in jail. . . . My brothers are dead. . . . My sisters. . . ? I don't know. Gone. . . ." She puts her hand over her mouth and does not look at her visitors.

21 "Then, why? Why go back?" asks Miss Green. "You're a beautiful, *brilliant* student and you'll finish your training in six months. . . . Why?"

22 Thi Nham Binh sighs. "I do not wish to die among strangers."

23 "Die?" asks Mrs. Nguyen.

24 Thi Nham Binh nods. "Yes. I have been dying for twenty-one months — since I left my family. I want to finish — end it — there, on my own earth, in my own way. Perhaps I will join my mother in jail, and we can give each other comfort and love."

25 "I'm afraid that is impossible," Miss Green says.

Cantonese — language spoken in China
landlady — one who rents rooms
brilliant — very intelligent

26 Thi Nham Binh smiles slowly. "That is what people said in Saigon twenty-one months ago. I told them I would escape. Impossible, they said. You will be caught. You will drown. The *pirates* will *rape* you and kill you. You will float on the sea for weeks and die of hunger and thirst. . . . None of those things happened. . . . You know my story, Miss Green. Yes?"

27 Miss Green *blushes* and says, "Well, actually, I'm not sure that I do — really — and I don't have your *file* here —"

28 "File? You don't need my file. You have **me**. I will tell you how I survived — and began to die."

29 "When the Americans left Saigon in their helicopters and airplanes, we knew the war would end. Saigon was very quiet. We couldn't hear the war anymore. There were no more rockets. No more fires, no more sounds of shooting in the streets. We waited and we were frightened. The North Vietnamese and the *Cong* came in — and the Russians. Life went on almost the way it was before the war. I received my *baccalaureate* at the university — in mathematics.

30 "Then, in 1977, things fell apart. We learned that my brothers had been killed. They were soldiers in the *ARVN*. We thought that they had escaped to Thailand, but no — they had been caught and killed. The shock of their deaths killed my father, I'm sure. He had a heart attack and died. The men in our family were gone.

31 "In Saigon, we were rich; we had a big house and three servants. You would call us middle-class here, I suppose. My father was an electrical engineer, and we lived well. After his death, the police came to see us — I think for two reasons; because my brothers had been soldiers and because someone in

---

pirate — robbers who use boats
rape — force someone to have sex
blushes — her face turns red
file — paper telling her history
Cong — North Vietnamese army
baccalaureate — Bachelor of Arts degree (French)
ARVN — South Vietnamese army

the new ruling class wanted our house. The police came and entered without knocking — at any time: day or night. They *interrogated* my mother many times.

32   "My mother decided that I must leave. She said, 'You are beautiful and clever. You can't stay here.' I refused to leave her and my two young sisters. Then one day, a North Vietnamese soldier tried to rape me in a park near my house. I fought him, I screamed, and some people came. He ran away. When my mother saw me and heard my story, she said, *'That settles it.* You're leaving.' I agreed to go.

33   "My mother arranged it. She discovered that a group would leave Saigon in two weeks. She learned the name of the boatman and went to find him in the boat colony along the Mekong River. It wasn't easy. At first the boatman denied any trip, but my mother convinced him that she was not an *informer*. Then he told her that the boat was full and that there was no space. She offered him her rings, a bracelet and a chain — all gold, all gifts from my father. He accepted and gave her his word that I could go.

34   The police were everywhere and we had to be very careful. During the next two weeks certain passengers brought Quang, the boatman, parts of an engine — one piece at a time. The boatman and his friends put the parts together. Other people brought gasoline in one gallon containers. The boatman filled two large *drums* with this gasoline. Others brought water during the last two days. No one brought food. We would not eat any food on the trip. Our *destination* was Indonesia, and the trip would take five days.

35   "On the day of departure, my mother, my sisters and I cried and embraced each other many times. Then I walked out of the house as though I were going shopping. I walked to the boat

---

interrogated — questioned
That settles it — That's enough
informer — someone who finds out things for the police
drums — metal containers
destination — place where one is going

colony and *boarded* a small sailboat. There were three other persons on board. We were all strangers. We were afraid, and we didn't look at each other.

36   "On that day in February, 1978, the bay was filled with small sailboats. Many of them were carrying passengers who were on their way to Quang's big boat. It was hidden in the jungle at the mouth of the Mekong River. When I saw it, *my heart sank*! It was forty feet long and ten feet wide. We were 120 passengers!"

---

boarded — got on
my heart sank — I was shocked

EXERCISES: PART I

Exercise A: Recalling the Reading

Read each statement below and decide whether it is *true* or *false*. If the statement is false, correct it to make a true statement.

1. Thi Nham Binh is a refugee from Indonesia.
2. Thi Nham Binh is happy to see her visitors.
3. Mrs. Kincaid is her counselor.
4. Thi Nham Binh has heart disease.
5. Thi Nham Binh speaks English poorly.
6. Thi Nham Binh has escaped from Vietnam.
7. The Vietnam War destroyed the family of Thi Nham Binh.
8. After the war ended, life in Saigon was wonderful.
9. The mother of Thi Nham Binh arranged for her daughter's escape.
10. Quang's big boat easily carried 120 passengers.

Exercise B: Analyzing Ideas

Choose correct statements to complete the sentences below. You may have more than one answer for some sentences.

1. Mrs. Kincaid calls Miss Green because
   a. Thi Nham Binh hasn't paid the rent.
   b. Thi Nham Binh has noisy parties.
   c. Thi Nham Binh hasn't left her room for two days.

2. Thi Nham Binh speaks
   a. Vietnamese
   b. Thai
   c. French
   d. Cantonese
   e. English

3. Thi Nham Binh wants to return to Saigon because
   a. she wants to die at home.
   b. she wants to live at home with her parents.
   c. she has an American boyfriend in Saigon.

4. Thi Nham Binh realizes that
   a. returning to Vietnam is impossible.
   b. her mother has remarried.
   c. her heart is broken.

5. When Thi Nham Binh's mother visited the boatman,
   a. he denied the trip at first.
   b. he disappeared with the money.
   c. he discovered that she was a police informer.

Survivor (Part II)

(continued)

"I want to forget that trip — *un cauchemar* — but I cannot. I still dream of it. We *stood* for five days and nights. There was no room to lie down. We slept sitting and standing up, and we slept very little. There was no covering over our heads to protect us from the sun and rain. We ate no food. Each day we were allowed one small can of water. The young children on board cried and begged for food, but there was no food. An old man died on the fifth day — just at the end of the trip. But we had some good fortune, too. The sea was very calm, and no pirates attacked us.

38   "Then on the last night, the boatman lost his way in the darkness. We could see land and smell it, but when the boatman steered toward the shore, the boat crashed against the rocks. It rolled on its side and we fell into the water. People were screaming and hanging onto each other. I began to swim away from the boat. I *deserted* the others — people drowning. I saved myself. . . . Was that right or wrong? I ask myself over and over. . . . And I don't know. . . .

39   "We were on a small island, and the people there came to help us. They welcomed us and fed us that night. The next morning, they helped us to bury our dead. Thirty people had

---

un cauchemar — a bad dream (French)
deserted — left; abandoned

drowned, and the boat was destroyed. The boatman was missing too. Perhaps he sank under the weight of the gold we gave him for our passage. . . .

40 "Two days later, three Indonesian ships came to take us to the big island, Java. There was a large *refugee camp* there — about one thousand Vietnamese people. The Catholic Relief Agency took care of us. They gave us materials to build shelters for ourselves. Twelve people lived in each shelter. They gave us rice and fish and vegetables to cook. The rice came from the United States.

41 "There were five American teachers there, giving classes in English. The classes were very large, so I decided to teach myself English. I borrowed some books from my teacher and studied English alone for ten hours a day. When the American interviewer arrived, I could speak a little English to him. Yes, I would like to go to the United States. Yes, I had a relative in California — a nephew of my mother. There were many other questions which I answered in my *mother tongue*. The interviewer was very kind. I had seen only American soldiers before. This man was different. He was gentle and polite, and he smiled often — like a Vietnamese.

42 "My mother's nephew agreed to be my *sponsor*, and I was allowed to emigrate to the United States. On the day before our departure, I bought some new clothes in Djakarta. My mother had given me two gold coins when I left Saigon. I traded them to buy my clothes and for U.S. dollars. Afterwards, I wept. Those coins were part of my mother's love — my last gift from her. . . .

43 "The trip to the United States was like a dream. I don't remember it clearly. We *picked up* more refugees in Thailand and in Hong Kong, where we stayed for one night in a big hotel. My room was so large, so quiet. . . . I lay in the hot water

refugee camp — a place for homeless people
mother tongue — Vietnamese
sponsor — someone who takes care of another person
picked up — collected

of the bathtub for two hours, just thinking and dreaming. . . . I slept most of the way to California. . . . Each time I woke up I saw my new clothes and my *name-tag*. . . . I knew I was real but I felt so unreal, and so tired, so empty. . . . As though my life were leaking out of me, and I felt smaller and lighter. . . . A little floating life in a big plane up there in the cold and empty sky. . . ."

44 Thi Nham Binh turns her head away and stops speaking.

45 Mrs. Nguyen says, "I must *compliment* you on your use of English. You express yourself very well. . . . Is there more that you want to tell us?"

46 Thi Nham Binh shrugs. "Miss Green knows what happened at the home of my mother's nephew."

47 Miss Green nods. "Yes. He treated you very badly — not like a relative at all."

48 "Not like a human being," says Thi Nham Binh. "He took my living allowance, made me live in his garage, made me clean and cook for him and his American wife. . . ." She shakes her head. "*Incroyable! Un vrai bête*. . . . And so I had to leave. . . . But you see, the *alternative* is loneliness, and loneliness is killing me. . . . It is a great sin that people who want to give love and receive love cannot do it. They can weep and *rage* but they cannot love. . . . People here are nice to me; you see, I am an *object of their pity*. . . . Something left over from the war. . . . I make them feel guilty, and so they are kind. But they cannot love me because I am strange and different. And I cannot love them because they will not permit it. . . . A *victim* is not allowed to love an *oppressor*. . . . Do you understand what I am trying to say?"

---

name-tag — identification
compliment — praise
Incroyable! Un vrai bête — Unbelievable! A real animal! (French)
alternative — other way to live
rage — become angry
object of their pity — someone they feel sorry for
victim — someone who is hurt
oppressor — someone who hurts others

49 Miss Green looks at the floor and nods slowly. "Yes," she say. "I do understand. . . . The question is, what can we do?" She looks up at Thi Nham Binh. "Do you think that you can complete your program?"

50 "Program?" Thi Nham Binh says. "Oh, yes, I can finish my program and get a job and be successful as a *computer programmer*. Is that what you want to know?"

51 "Yes," says Miss Green. "That is my responsibility to you - to help you to find satisfactory employment. . . . "

52 Thi Nham Binh stares at Miss Green for several seconds. "I see. . . . I understand. . . ." She rises from her chair. "We Vietnamese are very *hospitable*," she says, "and I would like to make some tea for you. And then," she adds, "we can discuss my program, my work and my future. Please accept my invitation."

53 "Thank you," says Miss Green.

54 "Thank you," says Mrs. Nguyen.

55 "I'm glad you're feeling better," says Miss Green.

56 But Thi Nham Binh has gone into the kitchen, and she doesn't hear what Miss Green says.

---

computer programmer — someone who works with computers
hospitable — kind to guests

EXERCISES: PART II

Exercise A: Recalling the Reading

Read each statement and decide whether it is *true* or *false*. If the statement is false, correct it to make a true statement.

1. On the trip to Indonesia, the passengers had no good fortune at all.
2. At the end of the trip, there was a shipwreck.
3. Thi Nham Binh saved the lives of thirty passengers.
4. Thi Nham Binh went to English classes for ten hours a day.
5. Thi Nham Binh came to America by ship.
6. Her sponsor treated her very well.
7. Thi Nham Binh found Americans to be nice and friendly.
8. She was successful in her computer programming course.

Exercise B: Analyzing Ideas

Choose the correct statements to complete the sentences below.

1. The trip to Indonesia was difficult
   a. because the boat was attacked by pirates.
   b. because there wasn't any food.
   c. because there wasn't enough space.

2. Thi Nham Binh deserted the victims of the shipwreck
   a. to save herself.
   b. because they were elderly and would die anyway.
   c. because she thought they could swim.

3. The people on the island
   a. killed the boatman for his money.
   b. helped the survivors.
   c. called the police.

4. Thi Nham Binh studied English by herself
   a. because the classes were too large.
   b. because she was a slow learner.
   c. because she loved her mother tongue.

5. Thi Nham Binh's experiences in America were difficult because
   a. America was the enemy of South Vietnam in the war.
   b. she couldn't learn English.
   c. loneliness was killing her.

6. At the end of the story, Miss Green can't help Thi Nham Binh because
   a. Thi Nham Binh says that she can't finish her program successfully.
   b. Thi Nham Binh is going home to Saigon.
   c. Miss Green doesn't know what to do.
   d. none of the above.

Exercise C: Understanding the Reading

1. Quickly read the entire story again. In one sentence, explain why Thi Nham Binh says to Miss Green, "I see . . . I understand . . . That is your responsibility to me . . ."

2. Identify the person(s) or thing(s) referred to in each phrase. Pay special attention to the words in **boldface**.
   a. "The **woman** who answers the door is short, gray-haired and middle-aged."
   b. "There is no medicine for **my** illness."
   c. "File? **You** don't need my file. **You** have me."
   d. "**He** had a heart attack and died."
   e. "**You** would call us middle-class here, I suppose."
   f. "**She** offered him her rings, a bracelet, and a chain — all gold, all gifts from my father."
   g. "**We** were afraid, and **we** didn't look at each other."
   h. "**They** gave us material to build shelters for ourselves."
   i. "**He** treated you very badly — not like a relative at all."
   j. "**I** do understand. . . . The question is, what can **we** do?"

Exercise D: Word Study

We use a large number of verbs to describe human actions and human feelings. Read the statement below. Try to match the verbs of action and feeling with the nouns that explain the *causes* of those actions or feelings. Please understand that the causes listed are *not the only ones* that match the verbs. Different situations provide different causes. Also the causes of actions in an English-speaking society may differ from those in other cultures.

1. Jane *blushed* when her mother asked about her boyfriend.
2. He *stared at* the beautiful woman for thirty seconds.
3. He *paced* back and forth, looking at his watch every minute or two.
4. She listened to her daughter's story and then *shook her head* vigorously.
5. I walked up to the other man and *shook* my finger in his face.
6. She saw me and *waved*.
7. I waved back at her and *grinned*.
8. He read her letter several times and then *frowned*.
9. During the second hour of the professor's lecture, the students began to *squirm* in their seats.
10. When she heard the news, her face grew pale and her hands began to *tremble*.

    a. negation
    b. embarrassment
    c. greeting
    d. fascination
    e. boredom

    f. nervousness
    g. shock
    h. pleasure
    i. anger
    j. displeasure

Exercise E: Questions for Discussion and Writing.

1. Thi Nham Binh tells us how she survived the war in Vietnam. Why does she want to return to her country now?
2. Do you think that Thi Nham Binh will survive in the United States? What does she tell her visitors about that?

3. Do you think that Miss Green and Mrs. Nguyen understood Thi Nham Binh? Will they be able to help her? How?
4. What do you think will happen next? Give reasons for your opinion.
5. Close your book and think about this reading. Write a paragraph which explains how this story relates to "The Bonfire and the Ants" in Unit 1: Fables.

Exercise F: Additional Activities

Write a brief passage using *one* of the following suggestions:

1. While Thi Nham Binh is in the kitchen, Miss Green and Mrs. Nguyen have a conversation. What do you think they say to each other? Construct a *dialogue* between these two women.
2. After Miss Green and Mrs. Nguyen leave, Thi Nham Binh writes a *letter* to her mother. (She writes in Vietnamese, of course, but you will write in English.) What does she tell her mother about her life and about the experience with Miss Green and Mrs. Nguyen?

LESSON 16

Going Home

The Writer

PETE HAMILL (1935-   )

Pete Hamill is a well-known journalist whose work appears in several daily newspapers in the United States. The story he tells here was used in the song "Tie A Yellow Ribbon To The Old Oak Tree." This song first became very popular in the United States in the mid-1970s. Then, during the period from November 1979 to January 1981, the song became a national symbol for Americans to welcome the release of the fifty-two men and women held hostage in Iran. Yellow ribbons came out again during America's participation in Operation Desert Storm in the Middle East during 1991.

The Reading

Spring comes slowly to the northeastern states — New England, New York, and New Jersey. Florida is usually sunny and warm. Students from eastern colleges and universities have an annual vacation — "spring break" or "Easter holiday" — that lasts a little more than a week. Many students "go south," and their destination is often Fort Lauderdale, Florida, a resort famous for its beaches and fine, warm weather.

Traveling by bus is probably the cheapest and safest way to travel in the United States. Some passengers bring their own food, but the bus makes "convenience stops" for meals and for bathroom use. Howard Johnson's is a chain of motels and dining rooms all over the United States.

SHARING EXPERIENCES

Compare your responses with those of your classmates.

❏ Have you ever traveled a long distance by bus or train? Where did you go? What kinds of people did you meet? Did you talk with them? What sights did you see?

❏ How do students travel in your country? Do they take long-distance buses? Why or why not?

❏ Why are people kidnapped and kept hostage? How long do they remain captives? When are they released? Do you think they have some of the feelings about going home as ex-convicts have when they return home from prison? Why or why not?

❏ How do families of convicts get along while someone in their family is in prison? How do they feel about their family member being released?

❏ What are some customary ways to symbolize that someone is being welcomed home after a long absence? Listen to "Tie a Yellow Ribbon to the Old Oak Tree." Have you heard this song before? What is the main message of the song?

Going Home

Pete Hamill

They were going to Fort Lauderdale, Florida. There were six of them, three boys and three girls, and they got on the bus at 34th Street, carrying sandwiches and wine in paper bags. They were dreaming of golden beaches and tides of the sea as the gray, cold spring of New York *vanished* behind them. Vingo was on the bus from the beginning.

2   As the bus passed through New Jersey, they began to notice that Vingo never moved. He sat in front of the young people, his dusty face *masking his age*, dressed in a plain

---

vanished — disappeared
masking his age — hiding his age; giving no clue about how old he was

brown suit that did not fit him. His fingers were stained from cigarettes and he chewed the inside of his lip a lot. He sat in complete silence.

3   Deep into the night, the bus pulled into a Howard Johnson's restaurant and everybody got off the bus except Vingo. The young people began to wonder about him, trying to imagine his life; perhaps he was a sea captain; maybe he had run away from his wife; he could be an old soldier going home. When they went back to the bus, one of the girls sat beside him and introduced herself.

4   "We're going to Florida," the girl said brightly. "You going that far?"

"I don't know," Vingo said.

"I've never been there," she said. "I hear it's beautiful."

"It is," he said quietly, as if remembering something he had tried to forget.

"You live there?"

"I was there in the Navy, Jacksonville."

"Want some wine?" she said. He smiled and took a *swig* from the bottle. He thanked her and *retreated again into his silence*. After a while, she went back to the others as Vingo *nodded in sleep*.

5   In the morning they awoke outside another Howard Johnson's and this time Vingo went in. The girl insisted that he join them. He seemed very shy, and ordered black coffee and smoked nervously, as the young people *chattered* about sleeping on beaches. When they went back on the bus, the girl sat with Vingo again. After a while, slowly and painfully, he began to tell his story. He had been in jail in New York for the last four years, and now he was going home.

6   "Are you married?"

---

swig — a large swallow
retreated again into his silence — became silent again
nodded in sleep — let his head fall forward
chattered — talked fast and noisily

"I don't know."

"You don't know?" she said.

7   "Well, when I was in jail I wrote to my wife. I said, 'Martha, I understand if you can't stay married to me.' I said I was gonna be away a long time, and that if she couldn't stand it, if the kids kept askin' questions, if it hurt her too much, well, she could just forget me. Get a new *guy* — she's a wonderful woman, really something — and forget about me. I told her she didn't have to write me *or nothing*, and she didn't. Not for three-and-a-half years."

8   "And you're going home now, not knowing?"

9   "Yeah," he said shyly. "Well, last week, when I was sure the *parole was coming through* I wrote her. I told her that if she had a new guy, I understood. But, if she didn't, if she would take me back she should let me know. We used to live in this town, Brunswick, and there's a great big oak tree just as you come into town. I told her if she would take me back, she should put a yellow handkerchief on the tree, and I would get off and come home. If she didn't want me, forget it; no handkerchief and I'd keep going on through."

"*Wow*," the girl said. "Wow."

10   She told the others, and soon all of them were in it, *caught up in* the approach of Brunswick, looking at the pictures Vingo showed them of his wife and three children. Now they were 20 miles from Brunswick, and the young people took over window seats on the right side, waiting for the approach of the great oak tree. Vingo stopped looking, *tightening his face* into the *ex-con's* mask, as if *fortifying* himself against still another

---

guy — (slang) man
or nothing — or anything else
parole was coming through — parole - freedom from prison; freedom was agreed to by the authorities
wow — (slang) an expression of surprise
caught up in — very interested in
tightening his face — made his face tense and expressionless
ex-con — **con** — convict; **ex** — former
fortifying — making strong

disappointment. Then it was ten miles, and then five, and the bus became very quiet.

11   Then suddenly all of the young people were up out of their seats, screaming and shouting and crying, doing small dances, shaking clenched fists in triumph and *exaltation*. All except Vingo.

12   Vingo sat there *stunned*, looking at the oak tree. It was covered with yellow handkerchiefs, 20 of them, 30 of them, maybe hundreds, a tree that stood like a *banner of welcome*, blowing and *billowing in the wind*. As the young people shouted, the old con slowly rose from his seat, holding himself tightly, and *made his way* to the front of the bus to go home.

---

exaltation — joy, great happiness
stunned — unable to move or react because of very strong emotional feelings
banner of welcome — flag
billowing in the wind — waving
made his way — moved along

EXERCISES

Exercise A: Recalling the Reading

Read each statement below and decide whether it is *true* or *false*. If the statement is false, correct it to make a true statement.

1. The people in the story were traveling on the bus from New York to Florida.
2. At first, Vingo did not talk to the young people.
3. Vingo was dressed in expensive clothes.
4. Vingo had been in jail for nearly a year.
5. Vingo was eager to join the group of young people when they stopped at the Howard Johnson's restaurant.
6. Vingo reluctantly told his story to one of the girls in the group.
7. Vingo's wife told him that she wanted to marry someone else.
8. Vingo's wife wrote him frequently while he was in jail.
9. Vingo didn't know if his wife wanted him to come home when he got out of jail.
10. Vingo told his wife to tie a red handkerchief to the old oak tree if she wanted him to come home.
11. The young people on the bus got very involved in watching for the oak tree.
12. When the bus stopped at Brunswick, Vingo got off.

Exercise B: Understanding the Reading

Summarize the main idea.

1. Quickly read the entire story again. In one sentence, explain why the young people were so excited when they got to Brunswick.

2. Identify the person(s) or thing(s) referred to in each phrase. Pay special attention to the words in **boldface**.

a. "**They** were dreaming of golden beaches and tides of the sea. . . ."
b. "**His** fingers were stained from cigarettes and **he** chewed the inside of **his** lip a lot."
c. ". . . perhaps **he** was a sea captain . . ."
d. "I hear **it's** beautiful."
e. "**He** had been in jail in New York for the last four years . . ."
f. ". . . if **she** couldn't stand it, if the kids kept askin' questions, if it hurt **her** too much, well, **she** could just forget me."
g. "And **you're** going home now, not knowing?"
h. "I told **her** if **she** would take me back, **she** should put a yellow handkerchief on the tree . . ."
i. ". . . took over window seats on the right side . . ."
j. ". . . slowly rose from **his** seat, holding **himself** tightly . . ."

Exercise C: Analyzing Ideas

Choose correct statements to complete the sentences below.

1. The young people on the bus were going to Florida because
   a. they wanted to vacation in the sunshine.
   b. it was their Christmas vacation.
   c. they went to school in Florida.

2. One thing that the young people noticed about Vingo was
   a. that he liked to meet new people.
   b. that he did not move or speak for a long time.
   c. that he was very old.

3. When the young people wondered about Vingo's life, they thought
   a. that he might have been a criminal.
   b. that he could have been a sea captain.
   c. that he could have been a very wealthy man.

4. When Vingo finally went into Howard Johnson's restaurant with the young people, he acted very
   a. shy.   b. angry.   c. relieved.

5. The young people on the bus found out about Vingo's story because
   a. Vingo told them himself.
   b. the girl that sat next to Vingo told them.
   c. they had heard about Vingo from the bus driver.

6. From Vingo's description of his letter to his wife, we can assume
   a. that he wanted her to forget about him.
   b. that he would be angry with her if she had remarried.
   c. that he wanted her to be happy.

7. Vingo asked his wife to let him know if
   a. she had remarried.
   b. she wanted him back.
   c. she still lived in Brunswick.

8. As the bus approached Brunswick, Vingo
   a. watched eagerly for a glimpse of the oak tree.
   b. became very animated and talked excitedly to the young people.
   c. tightened his face into a mask and prepared for a disappointment.

9. The young people shouted and cried as Vingo got off the bus because
   a. they were happy for Vingo.
   b. they felt sorry for Vingo.
   c. Vingo was leaving them.

10. The oak tree had lots of yellow handkerchiefs on it because Vingo's wife
    a. was worried that Vingo wouldn't be able to see just one handkerchief.
    b. wanted to show him how glad she was to have him home.
    c. wanted him to stay on the bus and keep going.

Exercise D: Informal Speech

When people speak easily and quickly with other people whom they know, we hear a kind of English speech that omits words and syllables. Pete Hamill's characters in "Going Home" sometimes speak in this informal way. In the story, find the examples of informal speech given below. In the space provided write the complete sentence that you think the speaker intended to say.

1. "You going that far?"

    _____

2. "You live there?"

    _____

3. "Want some wine?"

    _____

4. ". . . And she didn't. Not for three and a half years."

    _____

5. "If she didn't want me, forget it, no handkerchief. . . ."

    _____

Exercise E: Structure and Style

The following words are used as clause subordinators in this story: *if, after, when,* and *because.*

1. Rewrite the pairs of sentences listed below as single sentences using the clause subordinators listed. The pairs of sentences can be reordered before joining them as clauses, if necessary.
2. Reorder the sentences you have made so that the nine sentences record the sequence of events as they occurred in the story.

Example: The bus passed through New Jersey. The young
people noticed that Vingo hadn't moved.

After the bus had passed through New Jersey, the
young people noticed that Vingo hadn't moved

1. Vingo saw that the tree was covered with yellow
handkerchiefs. He sat there stunned.

   _____

2. Vingo had committed a crime. Vingo had been in jail for four
years.

   _____

3. The bus pulled into the restaurant. Everybody got off except
Vingo.

   _____

4. The bus stopped at Brunswick. The old con got off to go
home.

   _____

5. She wants me to come home. She should tie a yellow
handkerchief to the old oak tree.

   _____

6. The young people got back on the bus. One of the girls sat
beside him and introduced herself.

   _____

7. He was preparing himself for another disappointment.
Vingo tightened his face into an ex-con's mask.

   _____

8. They got on the bus. They were carrying sandwiches and
wine in paper bags.

   _____

9. Vingo told the girl his story. He showed the young people
some pictures of his wife and children.

   _____

Exercise F: Questions for Discussion and Writing

1. Why were the young people interested in Vingo?
2. Does it matter to you that you don't know exactly why Vingo was in jail? Why or why not?
3. Why didn't Vingo's wife write to him for three and a half years?
4. Why do you think Vingo's wife tied so many yellow handkerchiefs to the oak tree? What was her message to him?
5. What do you think that the young people would have said to Vingo if there had been no handkerchiefs on the tree?
6. Were you satisfied with the ending of the story? How did you feel?

Exercise G: Additional Activity

Maggie Phillips was the young woman who sat next to Vingo on the bus and heard his story. Maggie and Vingo exchanged home addresses before he got off the bus. He told Maggie he'd write her a letter. She doubted that he would, but he kept his word. When she returned to New York, there was a letter from Vingo waiting for her. It was a brief letter thanking her for her friendship and describing the events of his homecoming. After Maggie had read Vingo's letter, she telephoned each of her friends on the trip to Fort Lauderdale. Maggie read Vingo's letter aloud to them.

What did Vingo's letter say? It began by thanking Maggie for her friendship. Then it went on to describe his homecoming; his reunion with his wife and children after a four-year absence; his meeting with friends and neighbors; the "welcome home" dinner; and an invitation to Maggie and her friends to come by and say hello to Vingo and his family.

Write the kind of simple, brief letter you think Vingo would write to Maggie.

5

Visions

LESSON 17

I Have a Dream

The Writer

MARTIN LUTHER KING, JR. (1929-1968)

Americans became aware of the Civil Rights Movement in the southern United States through the Freedom Rides led by Martin Luther King, Jr. in Mississippi in the early 1960s. Like Langston Hughes, Martin Luther King, Jr. never used or proposed violence as a solution to the conflict between African Americans and whites in America. King was a preacher, and he preached nonviolent resistance as the way to get social equality and justice. In 1964, Dr. King received the Nobel Peace Prize for his nonviolent program in America.

M. L. King was murdered by a rifleman in Memphis, Tennessee. James Earl Ray, a white man and an escaped convict, pleaded guilty to the crime and was sentenced to nintey-nine years in prison. Martin Luther King's birthday is celebrated as a national holiday in America.

"I Have a Dream" is M. L. King's most famous sermon, which he presented on August 28, 1963, to 200,000 people who gathered before the Lincoln Memorial in Washington, D.C.

The Reading

One decade in American cultural history that will be studied for many years is the ten-year period we call "The Sixties." The reason for the study should be clear: many events took place, and some of them changed the course of American history in significant ways. The assassination of three American leaders — President John Kennedy, his brother, Robert, and Martin Luther King, Jr. — within five years, 1963 to 1968, is reason enough to study "The Sixties" carefully.

But there were other reasons. At home, there were strikes and marches in favor of civil rights for minorities. Abroad, there was almost a conflict between the United States and the (then) Soviet Union. And there was the American involvement in Vietnam.

In the midst of these violent conflicts there was the presence of a nonviolent African American preacher, Martin Luther King, Jr. His vision that the United States of America will "one day" be transformed into a nation of equality, liberty, and justice was expressed in thirty-three lines, placed on the page to look like poetry. Dr. King's sources for his sermon are the Declaration of Independence and the Christian Bible.

SHARING EXPERIENCES

Compare your responses with those of your classmates.

❑ In the last fifty years, has any minority group in your country fought wars or organized political demonstrations in an effort to achieve equality? What group was it? Who led the group? Did the group achieve its goal?

❑ Recall the selection from Maya Angelou's *I Know Why a Caged Bird Sings*. What did you learn from that reading about the situation of the African American in the South in the 1930s? How were African Americans treated differently from whites? What other things do you know about the situation of the African American in the South between 1930 and 1960?

❑ Share with your classmates what you learned in your country about Martin Luther King and the American Civil Rights Movement. When did Martin Luther King lead civil rights demonstrations in the United States? What was the goal of these demonstrations? Was King successful in achieving his goal?

I Have A Dream

Martin Luther King, Jr.

I have a dream
That one day
This nation will rise up
And live out the true meaning of its *creed*
"We hold these truths to be self-evident,
That all men are created equal."

I have a dream
That one day on the red hills of Georgia
The sons of former slaves
And the sons of former slave holders

---

creed — belief (from Latin, *credo* - I believe)
We hold . . . created equal — from the Declaration of Independence
(1776) before the United States was an independent country

Will be able to sit down together
At the table of human brotherhood.

I have a dream
That one day
Even the state of *Mississippi*
A state *sweltering* with the heat of oppression
Will be *transformed*
Into an *oasis* for freedom and justice.

I have a dream
That my four little children
Will one day live in a nation
Where they will not be judged
By the color of their skin
But by the content of their character.

I have a dream
That one day
Every valley shall be *exalted*
Every hill and mountain shall be made low,
The rough places will be made plain,
And the crooked place will be made straight,
And the glory of the Lord shall be revealed
And all *flesh* shall see it together.
This is our hope.

Mississippi — a southern state that supported slavery (until 1863)
sweltering — suffering from heat
transformed — changed
oasis — a cool, green place in the desert
exalted — raised to a high place, or to a high feeling
flesh — in this poem, refers to human kind

EXERCISES

Exercise A: Recalling the Reading

Read each statement below and decide whether it is *true* or *false*. If it is false, correct it to make a true statement

1. Martin Luther King led violent demonstrations to win rights for African Americans.
2. The statement "We hold these truths to be self-evident, That all men are created equal" is from the Constitution of the United States.
3. Martin Luther King was assassinated in 1968.
4. Georgia is a state in the northern Untied States.
5. Martin Luther King hoped for equality for all people in the United States.
6. At one time, African Americans were kept as slaves in the United States.
7. The state of Mississippi did not support slavery.
8. Martin Luther King had three children when he wrote this poem.
9. Martin Luther King did not believe in slavery.
10. When Martin Luther King wrote this poem, he felt that his children were judged by the color of their skin.

Exercise B: Understanding the Reading

Summarize the main idea.

1. Quickly read the entire poem again. In one sentence, tell your classmates how Martin Luther King wants his children to be judged.
2. Identify the persons or thing(s) referred to in each phrase. Pay special attention to the words in **boldface**.
   a. "And live out the true meaning of **its** creed . . ."
   b. "Will be able to sit down **together** . . ."
   c. "A **state** sweltering in the heat of oppression . . ."

d. ". . . **they** will not be judged by the color of **their** skin . . ."
e. "And **all flesh** shall see it together."

Exercise C: Analyzing Ideas

Choose correct statements to complete the sentences below.

1. The main goal of the Civil Rights Movement was
    a. to end slavery.
    b. to force Mississippi to give freedom to African Americans.
    c. to give African American citizens in the United States the same rights as white citizens.

2. The Civil Rights Movement began
    a. in the northern part of the United States.
    b. in the southern part of the United States.
    c. in the middle part of the United States.

3. Martin Luther King, Jr. used _____ methods in his fight to gain equal rights for African American citizens.
    a. militant
    b. violent
    c. nonviolent

4. The "sons of former slaves" are
    a. white Americans.
    b. African Americans.
    c. Mexican Americans.

5. "The table of human brotherhood" is an image in the poem used to mean that
    a. African Americans and whites will meet around a table to negotiate civil rights matters.
    b. All races will meet together as equals.
    c. African American and white leaders will have a meal together.

6. The state of Mississippi is mentioned because
   a. of the freedom of justice that is guarantee to African American citizens.
   b. of its oppression of African American citizens.
   c. it is in the desert.

7. At the time that Martin Luther King wrote this poem,
   a. African Americans were judged by their character rather than by the color of their skin.
   b. African Americans were judged in the same way as white people.
   c. African Americans were judged by the color of their skin rather than by their character.

8. African Americans are also called
   a. slaves.   b. Negroes.   c. slave-owners.   d. blacks.

9. Martin Luther King felt that
   a. the United States was living up to its creed of equality.
   b. the United States wasn't living up to its creed of equality.
   c. the creed of equality in the United States was unfair.

10. "Every valley shall be exalted/Every hill and mountain shall be made low . . ." The image in these lines refers to the idea of
    a. greater inequality among people.
    b. leveling of the landscape so that whites don't live on hills while African Alericans live in valleys.
    c. greater equality among people.

11. "The rough places will be made plain, /and the crooked places will be made straight . . ." These lines refer to
    a. the triumph of justice.
    b. an easier, more comfortable life.
    c. the repair of the roads in areas where African Americans live.

12. "And the glory of the Lord shall be revealed /And all flesh shall see it together." These lines mean
    a. all people will understand God's love and justice.
    b. God will appear to all people on earth as a glorious king.
    c. Someone will show us all what God looks like.

Exercise D: Word Study

The images in "I Have A Dream" are all related to the main theme of the poem; the dream of equality for the African American citizens of the United States. Match each image in Column A with the explanation of the image in Column B.

Column A

_____ 1. This nation will rise up

_____ 2. The rough places will be made plain

_____ 3. Four little African American children

_____ 4. The table of human brotherhood

_____ 5. An oasis in the desert

Column B

a. symbols of all African American people

b. A place of freedom in the midst of injustice

c. A place where all meet on equal basis

d. The people will demand something

e. justice will prevail

f. There will be a war

g. Symbols for all slaves

h. A place in Africa

Exercise E: Structure and Style: Part I

One way of joining two sentences which are closely related is to combine one of the statements within the other. This combination is possible when *one* of the sentences uses a verb like these: *know, think, believe, understand, tell, say, hope, dream, explain, feel, report.* In combinations like these, the *main* sentence (clause) looks like this:

He dreamed (something).

The *subordinate* (dependent) sentence (clause) looks like this:

Men would all be equal one day.

The *new* sentence combines the two like this:

*He dreamed **that** men would all be equal one day.*

Questions can use the same pattern.

Sentence 1: Do you believe (something)?

Sentence 2: Martin Luther King was a great speaker.

Sentence 3: ____ Do you believe that M. L. King was ____

a great speaker?

In the eight pairs of statements and questions that follow, combine the two sentences. You can reverse the order of the sentences if you think it's necessary.

1. Maria told her mother *(something)*. She liked Martin Luther King's poem.

   _____

2. His skin color is *not* important. Martin Luther King told him . . .

   _____

3. Many people are prejudiced. I have a feeling . . .

   _____

4. Someday he will be a free man. He hopes . . .

   _____

5. The Civil Rights Movement was successful. Do you think . . ?

   _____

6. Many people believe *(something)*. Martin Luther King was a great man.

   _____

7. Martin Luther King was assassinated. Did you know . . . ?

   _____

8. He believes *(something)*. Nonviolent demonstrations are effective.

   _____

Exercise F: Questions for Discussion and Writing

1. Martin Luther King uses personal, simple, and familiar images in "I Have a Dream." Where do you find examples of this imagery? Why do you think Dr. King used such language?
2. African Americans are one of several minority groups in the United States today. Name some other minority groups in the United States and discuss what you know about them.
3. What are some ways in which African Americans were discriminated against in the United States? (For example, what rights did white citizens have that African Americans did not have?)

4. What are some ways in which we can show a person that we don't want to associate with him or her without actually saying so?

5. Do you think that all citizens of a country should have the same basic rights regardless of the color of their skin, the amount of money they have, their social class, their sex, or their religion?

6. Dr. Martin Luther King made his speech in 1963. Do African Americans have more rights now than they did at that time? Do you think Dr. King's dream will come true?

7. Have you ever felt discriminated against? Describe the situation in which you felt that you were not being treated as well as other people.

8. Close your book and think about MLK's dream. Explain the meaning of this sentence from the *Declaration of Independence*, composed by the founders of the United States of America: "We hold these truths to be self-evident, that all men are created equal."

Exercise G: Additional Activities

1. Look through the pictures and written materials about the Civil Rights Movement. Describe the atmosphere in which the civil rights demonstrations took place. What role did the National Guard, local police, and sheriff's department take in these demonstrations? Who was Rosa Parks? Why is she important to the Civil Rights Movement?

2. Look at the materials and pictures about the life of Martin Luther King. What was his father's occupation? What was the name of his organization? Where did he lead demonstrations? What national political support did he have? How was he regarded in his state and community? How did he die?

3. Listen to the recording of Martin Luther King's speech which includes "I Have a Dream." What kind of voice did Dr. King have? Does his speech inspire you? How does the speech make you feel?

LESSON 18

The Last Night of the World

The Writer

RAY BRADBURY (1920–)

Ray Bradbury is a writer of science fiction — that kind of writing which invents worlds beyond the one we live in. But voyages into fantastic outer space are only one part of Bradbury's creation. He also travels into people's minds — into inner space, as we call it — into their fears, anxieties, and hopes.

Mr. Bradbury has been writing science fiction for more than forty years.

"The Last Night of The World" is from *The Illustrated Man*, a collection of Bradbury's writings about outer space and inner space.

The Reading

In his Nobel Prize acceptance speech, William Faulkner said, "There is only one question: When will I be blown up?" Ray Bradbury's husband and wife in "The Last Night of the World" decide that the world will end on October 19, 1989, "because it's the year when things are as they are all over the world. . . . Bombers on their schedules both ways across the ocean tonight . . . will never see land."

William Faulkner's speech was given in 1949. Ray Bradbury's story has a 1952 copyright. The date given for the world's end is 1989, thirty-seven years beyond 1952. The first printing of *Reflections* was 1979, thirty years after Faulkner's

Nobel Prize speech and ten years before Bradbury's vision of the world's end.

The date of this writing is 1993. There are over one hundred armed conflicts going on all over the world. But no one is talking about the end of the world or asking when a nuclear holocaust will take place. Instead, there are questions of another kind: How can we save the planet? How can we feed the hungry and look after the sick?

The troubles of a time — a decade, a generation, a century — will be reflected in a country's literature. Perhaps it is time now for writers to turn away from nuclear disaster and to write about other problems, other calamities, and new visions.

SHARING EXPERIENCES

Compare your responses with those of your classmates.

❏ All of us have routines from beginning and ending each day. Our routines for workday mornings and evenings are usually different from our weekend and holiday routines. Describe part of your routine or part of the routine of your housemate(s), spouse, parents, or other family members.

❏ Sometimes we can escape to familiar routines when traumatic events (such as natural disasters, sudden major illnesses, or sudden deaths) occur. These routines help us feel as if we are in control. Recall the last time that a traumatic event occurred in your life. What routine activity did you pursue while you tried to cope with the traumatic event?

❏ Think about what you would do if you knew the world were ending tomorrow. Write a list of things you would do in the next twenty-four hours.

- What sounds would you like to hear?
- What smells would you like to smell?
- What flavors would you like to taste?
- What people/things/scenes would you like to see?
- What textures and sensations would you like to feel?
- Whom would you like to be with?
- Where would you like to be?
- Share some things from your list with your classmates.

❑ In your homeland, do people talk about the end of the world? What do they say about it? How will the world end? What do some religions believe about the end of the world?

The Last Night of the World

Ray Bradbury

"What would you do if you knew that this was the last night of the world?"

"What would I do? You mean seriously?"

"Yes, seriously."

"I don't know. I hadn't thought."

2   He poured some coffee. In the background, the two girls were playing *blocks* on the *parlor* rug in the light of the green

---

blocks — a young children's game of stacking wooden blocks together

parlor — reception room or living room of the house

hurricane lamps. There was an easy, clean *aroma* of the *brewed coffee* in the evening air.

"Well, better start thinking about it, " he said.

"You don't mean it!"

He nodded.

"A war?"

He shook his head.

"Not the hydrogen or *atom bomb*?"

"No."

"Or *germ warfare*?"

"None of those at all," he said, stirring his coffee slowly. "But just, let's say the *closing of a book*."

"I don't think I really understand."

3   "No, nor do I, really; it's just a feeling. Sometimes it frightens me; sometimes I'm not frightened at all but at peace." He glanced in at the girls and their yellow hair shining in the lamplight. "I didn't say anything to you. It first happened four nights ago."

"What?"

4   "A dream I had. I dreamed that *it was all going to be over*, and a voice said it was; not any kind of voice I can remember, but a voice anyway, and it said it was going to stop here on Earth. I didn't think too much about it until the next day but then I went to the office and caught Stan Willis looking out the window in the middle of the afternoon, and I said, '*A penny for your thoughts*, Stan,' and he said, 'I had a dream last night,' and before he even

---

hurricane lamp — lamp which has candles inside
aroma — odor, smell
brewed coffee — freshly made coffee
atom bomb — a bomb whose explosive force can destroy a whole city
germ warfare — a method of war in which germs deadly to man are used as weapons
closing of a book — the end of a story or chain of events; the end of life
it was all going to be over — (it – life) life was going to be finished
a penny for your thoughts — asking someone to tell what he's thinking

told me I knew what it was. I could have told him, but he told me and I listened to him."

5   "It was the same dream?"

"The same. I told Stan I had dreamed it too. He didn't seem surprised. He relaxed, in fact. Then we started walking through the office, *for the hell of it*. It wasn't planned. We didn't say 'Let's walk around.' We just walked on our own, and everywhere we saw people looking at their desks, or their hands or out windows. I talked to a few. So did Stan."

6   "And they all had dreamed?"

"All of them. The same dream, with no difference."

"Do you believe in it?"

"Yes. I've never been more certain."

"And when will it stop? The world, I mean."

7   "Sometime during the night for us, and then as the night goes on around the world, that'll go too. It'll take twenty-four hours *for it all to go*."

8   They sat while not touching their coffee. Then they lifted it slowly and drank, looking at each other.

"Do we *deserve* this?" she said.

"It's not a matter of deserving; it's just that things didn't *work out*. I noticed you didn't even argue about this. Why not?"

"I guess I've a reason," she said.

"The same one everyone at the office had?"

9   She nodded slowly. "I didn't want to say anything. It happened last night. And the women on the block talked about it, among themselves, today. They dreamed. I thought it was only *coincidence*." She picked up the evening paper. "There's nothing in the paper about it."

"Everyone knows, so there's no need."

---

for the hell of it — (slang) for no good reason
for it all to go — (it – the world) for the world to be destroyed
deserve — to be suitably punished or rewarded with something
work out — happen in the right way
coincidence — happening at the same time by chance

He sat back in hs chair, watching her. "Are you afraid?"

"No. I always thought I would be, but I'm not."

"What's that spirit called *self-preservation* they talk so much about?"

"I don't know. You don't get too excited when you feel things are *logical*. Nothing else but this could have happened from the way we lived."

"We haven't been too bad, have we?"

10 "No, nor enormously good. I suppose that's the trouble — we haven't been very much of anything except us, while a big part of the world was busy being lots of quite awful things."

The girls were laughing in the parlor.

"I always thought people would be screaming in the streets at a time like this."

"I guess not. You don't scream about the real thing."

11 "Do you know, I won't miss anything but you and the girls. I never liked cities or my work or anything except you three. I won't miss a thing except perhaps the changes in the weather, and a glass of ice water when it's hot, and I might miss sleeping. How can we sit here and talk this way?"

12 "Because there is nothing else to do."

"That's it, of course; for if there were, we'd be doing it. I suppose for the first time in the history of the world that everyone has known just what they were going to do during the night."

"I wonder what everyone else will do now, this evening, for the next few hours."

"Go to a show, listen to the radio, watch television, play cards, put the children to bed, go to bed themselves, like always."

"In a way that's something to be *proud of* — like always."

---

self-preservation — protecting oneself from harm or destruction
logical — orderly and reasonable
proud of — happy or pleased with

13 They sat a moment and then he poured himself another coffee. "Why do you suppose *it's tonight?*"

"Because."

"Why not some other night in the last century, or five centuries ago, or ten?"

14 "Maybe it's because it was never October 19, 1989, ever before in history, and now it is and that's it; because it's the year when things are as they are all over the world and that's why it's the end."

15 "There are bombers on their schedules both ways across the ocean tonight that'll never see land."

"That's part of the reason why."

"Well," he said, getting up, "what shall it be? Wash the dishes?"

16 They washed the dishes and *stacked* them away with special neatness. At eight-thirty the girls were put to bed and kissed good night and the little lights by their beds turned on and the door left open *just a trifle.*

"I wonder," said the husband, coming from the bedroom and glancing back, standing there with his pipe for a moment.

"What?"

"If the door will be shut all the way, or if it'll be left just *a little ajar* so some light comes in."

"I wonder if the children know."

"No, of course not."

17 They sat and read the paper and talked and listened to some radio music and then sat together by the fireplace watching the *charcoal embers* as the clock struck ten-thirty and eleven and eleven-thirty. They thought of all the other people in

---

it's tonight — (it – the end of the world)
stacked — placed one on top of another
just a trifle — small amount
a little ajar — slightly open
charcoal embers — the remains of a fire

the world who had spent their evening, each in his own special way.

"Well," he said at last.

He kissed his wife for a long time.

"We've been good for each other, anyway."

"Do you want to cry?" he asked.

"I don't think so."

18   They moved throught the house and turned out the lights and went into the bedroom and stood in the night's cool darkness undressing and pushing back the covers.

"The sheets are so clean and nice."

"I'm tired."

"We're *all* tired."

They got into bed and lay back.

"Just a moment,"she said.

19   He heard her get out of bed and go into the kitchen. A moment later, she returned. "I left the water running in the sink." she said.

Something about this was so very funny that he had to laugh. She laughed with him, knowing what she had done was funny. They stopped laughing at last and lay in their cool bed, their hands *clasped*, their heads together.

"Good night," he said, after a moment."Good night," she said.

---

clasped — tightly held each other's hand

EXERCISES

Exercise A: Recalling the Reading

Read each staement below and decide whether it is *true* or *false*. If the statement is false, correct it to make it a true staement.

1. The conversation between the couple in this story takes place in the morning.
2. The couple's two sons are playing in the room where they are talking.
3. The husband and wife have both had the same dream about the end of the world.
4. The couple's friends and acquaintances have had dreams about the end of the world that are different from theirs.
5. On October 19, 1989 (when this story takes place), there are wars going on in the world.
6. The husband says he will miss his work and the city life when the world ends.
7. The husband and wife decide to follow their usual evening routine on this last night.
8. Outside of their home, they can hear people screaming in the streets.
9. The husband and wife both seem content with the life they've led.
10. The wife cries herself to sleep on this last night.

Exercise B: Understanding the Reading

Summarize the main idea.

1. Quickly read the entire story again. In one sentence tell what the man will miss when the world ends.

2. Identify the person(s) ot thing(s) referred to in each phrase. Pay special attention to the words in **boldface**.
   a. "**I** don't know. **I** hadn't thought."
   b. "Sometimes **it** frightens **me**, sometimes **I'm** not frightened at all but at peace."

c. "... it said **things** would stop here on Earth."

d. "**He** didn't seem surprised. **He** relaxed, in fact."

e. "Do **we** deserve this?"

f. "**They** dreamed. I thought it was only a coincidence."

g. "I suppose this is the first time in the history of the world that ... has known just what they were going to do during the night."

h. "At eight-thirty the ... were put to bed and kissed good night ..."

i. "They thought of all of the ... in the world who had spent **their** evening, each in his own special way."

j. "**They** stopped laughing at last and lay in their cool bed, **their** hands clasped, their heads together."

Exercise C: Analyzing Ideas

Choose the best answers for the statements and questions below.

1. Who had the dream first?

    a. The wife did.

    b. The husband and his fellow workers did.

    c. The women on the block did.

    d. Everyone had the dream the same night.

2. How did the husband and wife feel about the end of the world?

    a. angry.   c. happy.

    b. resigned.   d. afraid.

3. The couple

    a. did something special the last night.

    b. did the same things as usual the last night.

    c. prepared for the end on their last night.

    d. worried about the children on their last night.

4.

Although they did not say so directly, the couple implied that

    a. there was no warfare in the world.

    b. their country was at war.

    c. all countries were at peace with each other.

    d. there was warfare somewhere in the world.

5. The conversation of the couple indicates that
   a. they have been very concerned about affairs in the rest of the world.
   b. they haven't paid much attention to affairs in the rest of the world.
   c. they have discussed the end of the world with their children.
   d. they feel a need to find out the details of the event that they are expecting.

6. The couple felt that the world
   a. should have ended long ago.
   b. didn't deserve to end.
   c. was ending because it was the natural time.
   d. wasn't really going to end.

7. The couple laughed after the wife got up to turn off the water in the kitchen because
   a. it was such an ordinary concern on such an extraordinary night.
   b. she usually left the water running all night.
   c. it was such an unusual thing to do.
   d. they were very happy that this was their last night in the world.

Exercise D — Part One: Word Study: Vocabulary Extension

Below is a list of words from "The Last Night of the World." Complete each of the sentences from the story by supplying the correct forms of the appropriate words from this list.

miss	background	touch	pour
play	hell	struck	block
caught	mean	enormous	spirit

1. We feel _____ grateful to him for all his kindness.

2. All of the women on the _____ talked about their dream.

3. I _____ Stan Willis looking out the window and I said, "A penny for your thoughts, Stan."

4. In the _____ the two girls were _____ blocks.

5. That's it; maybe this day _____ more than any other day ever did.

6. I won't _____ a thing except the changes in the weather.

7. They were so deep in discussion that they didn't _____ the coffee they had poured.

8. Where's that _____ called self-preservation?

9. He relaxed; then we started walking through the office for the _____ of it.

10. He _____ himself another coffee and said, "Why do you suppose it's tonight?"

11. They sat by the fireplace watching the charcoal embers as the clock _____ ten-thirty.

12. The two girls were playing _____ on the parlor rug.

Exercise D — Part Two: Word Study: Vocabulary Extension

Choose words from the list in Part I to complete the sentences below. You will notice that the words have different meanings in these sentences than they did in the sentences in Part I. As you will discover, the meanings of these words change when the contexts for their use change.

1. Does the _____ live on after the body dies?

2. The lion _____ his paw in the trap.

3. The rain _____ down for days and the fields turned to mud.

4. That word _____ the same as this one.

5. He's so close to the target that he can't possibly _____ it.

6. The falling rocks _____ the man on the head.

7. Christians believe that people's souls go to heaven or
   _____ after they die.

8. He _____ the part of the king in that production of
   Hamlet.

9. I would like to study law, but I don't have the _____
   for it.

10. The road was _____ off because of the construction
    project.

11. The blind girl _____ my face when I was introduced
    to her.

12. An _____ shark swam though the waves just fifty
    yards from the shore.

Exercise E: Structure and Style

Wrtie a sentence from the story which relates to each of the senses
listed below:

1. Sight _____

2. Smell _____

3. Touch _____

4. Hearing _____

5. Taste _____

Exercise F: Questions for Discussion and Writing

1. Do you think that the couple in the story are very concerned
   about the people in the world outside their family? Find
   sentences in the story to support your answer.

2. Do you believe that the children knew it was the last night of
   the world? Find sentences to support your answer.

3. How did the family in the story spend the last night of the
   world?

4. Why do you suppose that the couple in the story said
   "Good-night" to each other instead of "Good-bye"?

5. Why do you think the couple is so *passive*? Why aren't they angry or sad or depressed?

6. Why do you think the husband and wife spend their last night doing what they always do?

7. Do you think that the husband and wife really *believe* that the world will end that night? What makes you think so?

8. Close your book and think about this story. Explain what the man in the story meant by this statement: "I suppose that's the trouble — we haven't been very much of anything except us, while a big part of the world was busy being lots of quite awful things."

Exercise G: Additional Activity

At the end of the story, we don't know what will happen. Maybe the world will end as the dream said it would. Then again, maybe it won't. Suppose at dawn the following morning, the husband woke up. He saw that the sun was shining. He heard the songs of birds and a dog barking somewhere. He got up and went to the window and looked out. Finish the story as you like.

LESSON 19

Nobel Prize Acceptance Speech

The Writer

WILLIAM FAULKNER (1897–1962)

William Faulkner was one of those remarkable writers who wrote about a region, a particular place from which he saw the world; and at the same time, his writing had a universal appeal. Faulkner was in one sense a "southern writer" because his stories and novels are rooted in the southern U.S., in a place Faulkner invented: Yoknapatawpha County (the accent falls on the -*taw*-) in Mississippi. In a larger sense, Faulkner, like other regional American writers Robert Frost, John Steinbeck, and Mark Twain, wrote for the world.

In 1949, when he won the Nobel Prize in Literature, his acceptance speech was brief and eloquent. In the last years of his life Faulkner wrote to a friend: ". . . What an amazing gift I had: uneducated in every formal sense . . . yet to have made the things I made. I don't know where it came from . . . I don't know why God . . . [made] me the vessel. . . ."

There is an American proverb: "Practice what you preach." From the beginning of his career, Faulkner had written "the old verities and truths of the heart . . " in his stories and novels.

The Reading

The Nobel Prize in Literature is one of six prizes (the others are in physics; chemistry; physiology and medicine; international peace; and economic science) that are awarded annually to persons of any nationality.

The Nobel prizes carry the name of their founder, Alfred Nobel (1833–1896), a Swedish chemist who invented dynamite, among other substances, and became extremely rich. He suffered from guilt because he had invented a product that caused great injury to people and their environment.

The Nobel Prize in Literature is presented by the Royal Swedish Academy to an author whose entire works have "proved by the test of experience or by the examination of experts" to occupy a unique place in the world of letters.

SHARING EXPERIENCES

Compare your responses with those of your classmates.

❏ Have you ever received an award for a special achievement? If so, how did you feel when you received the award? Did you make a speech? What kinds of things did you say in your speech?

❏ Can you name anyone who has received the Nobel Prize besides Faulkner?

❏ Make two personal lists. On one list, use the heading "Things that give me hope" and on the other write "Things that make me fearful".

Put each of the words or phrases below under one of the headings: injury, sickness, good health, love, hate, medical care, nuclear weapons, war, peace, human achievements, courage, cowardice, earthquakes, sunshine.

❏ Do you believe in the human spirit and the human soul? Do you believe that the soul lives on after the body dies? Why or why not?

Acceptance Speech

William Faulkner

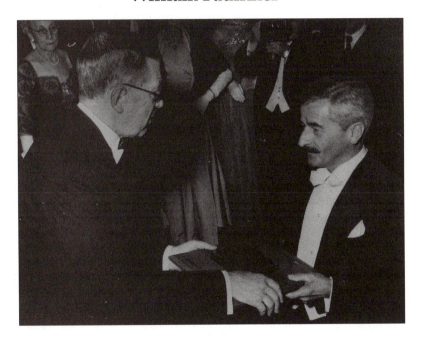

I feel that this award was not made to me as a man, but to my work — a life's work in the *agony* and sweat of the human spirit, not for the glory and least of all for the profit, but to create out of the materials of the human spirit something which did not exist before. So this award is mine only *in trust*. It will not be

---

agony — here, struggle
in trust — to be cared for; to look after but not to own

difficult to find a *dedication* for the money part of it *commensurate with* the purpose and *significance* of its origin. But I would like to do the same with the *acclaim*, too, by using this moment as a *pinnacle* from which I might be listened to by the young men and women already *dedicated* to the same *anguish and travail*, among whom is already that one who will some day stand here where I am standing.

2   Our *tragedy* today is a general and universal physical fear so long *sustained* by now that we can even *bear* it. There are no longer problems of the spirit. There is only the question: When will I be blown up? Because of this, the young man or woman writing today has forgotten the problems of the human heart in conflict with itself which alone can make good writing because only that is worth writing about, worth the agony and the sweat.

3   He must learn them again. He must teach himself that the *basest* of all things is to be afraid; and, teaching himself that, forget it forever, leaving no room in his workshop for anything but the old *verities and truths of the heart*, the old universal truths, lacking which story is *emphemeral* and *doomed* — love and honor and pity and pride and *compassion* and sacrifice. Until he does, he *labors under a curse*. He writes not of love but of *lust*, of defeats in which nobody loses anything of value, of victories without hope and, worst of all, without pity or compassion. His griefs grieve on no

---

dedication — here, worthy use
commensurate with — equal to
significance — meaning; importance
acclaim — praise and fame
pinnacle — high place
dedicated — here, devoted to
anguish and travail — pain and hard work
tradgedy — great sorrow
sustained — kept going
bear — here, endure; accept
basest — worst; lowest
verities and truths of the heart — necessary truths and beliefs
ephemeral — quickly gone; shortlived
doomed — sure to die
compassion — sympathy; desire to help
labors under a curse — works to no purpose
lust — sexual pleasure

universal bones, leaving no *scars*. He writes not of the heart but of the *glands*.

4   Until he learns these things, he will write as though he stood among and watched the end of man. I *decline* to accept the end of man. It is easy enough to say that man is *immortal* simply because he will *endure*: that when *the last dingdong of doom has clanged and faded* from the last worthless rock hanging *tideless* in the last red and dying evening, that even then there will still be one more sound: that of his *puny inexhaustible* voice, still talking. I refuse to accept this. I believe that man will not *merely* endure: he will *prevail*. He is immortal, not because he alone among creatures has an inexhaustible voice, but because he has a soul, a spirit capable of compassion and sacrifice and endurance. The poet's, the writer's, duty is to write about these things. It is his *privilege* to help man endure by lifting up his heart, by reminding him of the courage and honor and hope and pride and compassion and pity and sacrifice which have been the glory of his past. The poet's voice need not merely be the record of man, it can be one of the *props*, the *pillars* to help him endure and prevail.

---

universal bones — (figurative) large human problems
scars — (figurative) signs of injury
glands — here, something passing and unimportant
decline — refuse
immortal — undying
endure — continue; last; remain
the last dingdong of doom has clanged and faded — the end of the world has come
tideless — without tide; that is, dried up
puny — small; weak
inexhaustible — continual; untiring
merely — here, only
prevail — win; triumph
privilege — here, special ability or skill
props — supports
pillars — main columns that support a building

EXERCISES

Exercise A: Word Study: Negatives

William Faulkner in his Acceptance Speech does something strange and difficult. He presents a *positive* message to young writers of literature, but he uses many *negatives* to do this.

Work through the four paragraphs of Faulkner's speech; underline or list the negatives that you find. Some negatives like *no* and *not* are easy to find. Don't ignore others: words that end in *-less* or begin with *im-*. And there are words whose definitions suggest negation, too, or combine with other words to form negatives (words like *only* and *merely*).

Exercise B: Understanding the Reading

Summarize the main idea.

1. Quickly read the entire speech again. In one sentence, tell your classmates why Faulkner believes that man will prevail.

2. Identfiy the person(s) or thing(s) referred to in each phrase. Pay special attention to the words in **boldface**.

   a. "So **this** . . . is only mine in trust."

   b. ". . . among **whom** is already that one who will some day stand here where I am standing."

   c. "When will **I** be blown up?"

   d. ". . . because only **that** is worth writing about, worth the agony and the sweat."

   e. "**He** must teach **himself** that the basest of all things is to be afraid . . "

   f. "It is **his** privilege to help man endure by lifting his heart . . ."

Exercise C: Questions for Discussion and Writing

1. How does Faulkner decide to use his great moment in history?
2. Faulkner received the Nobel Prize in Literature in 1949, four years after the atomic bombing of Hiroshima and Nagasaki. How does his speech reflect those terrible events?
3. What must writers learn to do?
4. If writers don't learn and relearn "these things," how will their writing suffer and fail?
5. What must writers do to help humankind?
6. Do you think that Faulkner was optimistic or pessimistic about the future of human beings? Thus far, has history proved Faulkner right or wrong?

Exercise D: Additional Activity

How would you complete these statements, which summarize Faulkner's advice to young writers?

1. Write not for _____ but to create something out of the _____ that did not exist before.

2. Do not be _____ .

3. Leave no room for anything but _____ .

4. Write from the _____ not from the _____.

5. Humankind is not _____ because people _____ but because they will _____ .

6. Humans not only have (a) _____ but they also have _____.

7. Writers must not only inform and entertain readers, but they must _____ people of the old _____

_____ , as well.

8. Writers must not only _____ human lives and human history, they must keep humankind to _____ and

_____ .

Exercise E: Additional Activity

After reading William Faulkner's advice to writers and his belief in the value of literature, which *one* of the reading selections in *Reflections* would you choose as a good example of Faulkner's description of "good writing:" work that expresses the spirit, work that tells the "old verities and truths of the heart."

Write a brief passage explaining the reasons that you chose this work.

Appendix A

Teachers' Notes

UNIT 1: FABLES OLD AND NEW

THE DONKEY IN THE LION'S SKIN

CONTEXT BUILDING: *Objectives*: 1) To lead learners from a literal understanding of the setting and action of the story to an understanding of the moral: "He who pretends to be something he's not will always, sooner or later, give away the truth"; 2) to help learners imagine the action of the story by expanding their English vocabulary for animal names, descriptions and sounds. **SUGGESTED MATERIALS:** 1) Pictures of farm animals; 2) Flash cards with English words for animal sounds; 3) Tapes or records of animal sounds; 5) Flash cards with words describing animal bodies (See answer key); 6) Pictures of people in costume (e.g., Halloween, Mardi Gras, parades); 7) Optional: costumes for learners to try on.

THE MILKMAID AND HER PAIL

CONTEXT BUILDING: *Objective*: To lead learners from a literal understanding of the setting and action of the story to an understanding of the moral: "Don't count your chickens before they're hatched." **SUGGESTED MATERIALS:** Modern and dated pictures of farm life, transporting food to market, and market places in urban and rural areas, including open markets or farmers' markets. Optional items: fresh eggs, a plastic pail or basket to balance on one's head, some hats and scarves to model for admirers.

THE BONFIRE AND THE ANTS

CONTEXT BUILDING: *Objectives*: 1) To lead learners to an understanding of the central metaphor of the story: refugees, like ants, return to their war-torn homelands; 2) to help learners understand the experience of watching the ants flee from and then return to the bonfire by using sensory stimuli as well as visual images. **SUGGESTED MATERIALS:** 1) A video, slide, or photograph of ants swarming; 2) A piece of red cellophane; 3) A can of soda pop; 4) A video, slide, or photo of a campfire or bonfire

THE UNICORN AND THE GARDEN

CONTEXT BUILDING: *Objectives*: To help learners understand the physical setting (looking out at the garden from a breakfast nook) and the psychological setting (myth, husband-wife relationships) for this story. **SUGGESTED MATERIALS:** 1) Garden catalogs or picture books of gardens and flowers; 2) Pictures of unicorns, horses, oryxes, and antelopes; 3) Pictures of other mythical beasts: dragon, griffin, phoenix, mermaid, etc.; 4) Articles and/or pictures about psychiatry, mental hospitals, and mental health clinics; 5) Comic strips about husband-wife relationships: Dagwood and Blondie, For Better or For Worse, The Lockhorns, Sally Forth, etc.

UNIT 2: SORROWS

A WHITE MAN'S WORD

CONTEXT BUILDING: *Objectives*: 1) To help learners understand the variety of tribes represented among Native Americans, some of their cultural heritage, and the contrast between the size of past and present tribal land holdings; 2) to help learners understand the destructive effects of ethnic prejudice on individual self-esteem and group pride. **SUGGESTED MATERIALS:** Picture books about Native Americans, past and present. Good resources: Smithsonian Museum publications.

THE GEESE

CONTEXT BUILDING: *Objectives*: 1) To help learners understand the life rhythms of the fowl in the farmyard; 2) to help learners understand the relationship between the author's life cycle and his commentary on the plight of the old gander. **SUGGESTED**

MATERIALS: Pictures of barnyard fowl and chicks hatching. Good resources include children's picture dictionaries, ESL picture dictionaries, Audubon books, and David Sharp's *Looking Inside the Wonders of Nature* (Chicago: Rand McNally, 1976).

THANK YOU, MA'M

CONTEXT BUILDING: *Objective*: To help learners understand these sociological and psychological issues in the story: urban life, street crime, the absence of a strong home life for young people from poor families, and the role of older generations in guiding younger members of a community. **SUGGESTED MATERIALS:** Purses and wallets of learners in the class; pictures of urban and small town life. Good resources: *A Day in the Life of America* and photos from both urban and small town newspapers.

YOU GO YOUR WAY, I'LL GO MINE

CONTEXT BUILDING: *Objectives*: 1) To help learners understand how the form and delivery of a message can affect the way in which the message is received; 2) to stimulate learners to think about cultural differences in the ways in which war and families are regarded; 3) to acquaint learners with the Mexican population in the United States. **SUGGESTED MATERIALS:** 1) A sample of telegrams or photocopies of telegrams and pictures of urban messengers in trucks, cars, on bicycles, and on foot; 2) pictures of war memorials in the United States, an American flag at half mast, and pictures of families holding photos of dead soldiers. Good resources: pictorial tourist guides to Washington, D. C., and newspaper stories published around Veteran's Day; 3) pictures of the Mexican American community in the United States. Good resources: *Life* and *Time* magazine issues with cover stories on this community.

UNIT 3: MEMORIES

ANTONIO'S FIRST DAY OF SCHOOL

CONTEXT BUILDING: *Objectives*: 1) To facilitate the identification of common memories of learners' first days at school; 2) to help learners who are studying English outside of their native countries share their feelings of loneliness and difference and gain common strength in their shared experiences; 3) to help learners use their own memories to understand Antonio's feelings in this story; 4) to help learners understand the geographical and social setting of this story. **SUGGESTED MATERIALS**: 1) Pictures of Young children going to school or attending school. Good resources include local newspapers and national magazines for the week after Labor Day — the first Monday in September; 2) examples of different writing systems and gestures; 3) a map of the United States and travel pictures of New Mexico. Good resources include airline magazines and New Mexico Chamber of Commerce brochures. **PROCESS:** 1) Have learners form small groups to share and discuss their memories. Encourage them to find common experiences. Each group can select a person to report common experiences from their group to the rest of the class. 2) Regroup learners to ensure a mixture of nationalities in each small group when they discuss feelings of differences. Use the same discussion and reporting process as was followed above. Circulate among groups to find out how learners' feelings of isolation may be affecting their learning of English.

GEORGE WASHINGTON, MY COUNTRYMAN

CONTEXT BUILDING: *Objectives*: 1) To help learners articulate the qualities of patriotism; 2) to determine how much learners know about American history; 3) to evoke feelings about freedom and citizenship in learners which will help them understand the feelings of the author; 4) to help learners undersatnd poetry as a way of sharing feelings with others. **SUGGESTED MATERIALS:** 1) Pictures of patriots from students' native countries (supplied by them); 2) pictures of George Washington, Benjamin Franklin, Dolly Madison, and other American patriots. Good resources include illustrated American history books; 3) a copy of the American Constitution and practice citizenship tests; 4) examples of American patriotic poetry (e.g., some of Walt Whitman's poems to America).

CHINESE SCHOOL

CONTEXT BUILDING: *Objectives*: 1) To help learners distinguish between individual differences and cultural differences in teacher behavior; 2) to prompt learners to talk about their own feelings as language learners and lead them to apply those feelings to the author's reaction to Chinese school.   **SUGGESTED MATERIALS:** None are necessary, but a picture of a Chinese classroom in the United States about 1960 would help comprehension.

Music Lady

CONTEXT BUILDING: *Objectives*: 1) To help learners recognize and name a variety of musical instruments; 2) to introduce students to (or enhance their knowledge of) a variety of Western classical music (especially by composers named in the story); 3) to introduce students to or enhance their knowledge of a variety of jazz styles (particularly, big band sounds like those of Stan Kenton; jazz vocalists like Billie Holiday, and ragtime pianists like Scott Joplin); 4) to help learners see the relationship between music and inspiration for a poet; 5) to evoke students' own childhood experiences with favorite haunts and adults who encouraged them.   **SUGGESTED MATERIALS:** 1) Pictures of musical instruments named in the exercise item; 2) examples of classical music by Bach, Beethoven, Hayden, and Mozart; 3) examples of jazz music described in the story: Big Band (by Stan Kenton), Billie Holiday's recordings (especially "Strange Fruit"); and Scott Jolpin's "Maple Leaf Rag"; 4) a recording of "Peter and the Wolf"; 5) interior pictures of record stores from the 1950s and 1960s.

UNIT 4: TIES

I Know Why the Caged Bird Sings

CONTEXT BUILDING: Objective: To build learners' understanding of the cultural, economic, social, and psychological setting of the first volume of Ms. Angelou's autobiography so that they may understand the words and actions of the characters in this reading.   **SUGGESTED MATERIALS:** 1) Pictures of American families small towns, including towns in the rural south, from the Depression era. Good resources include Martin J. Dain, *Faulkner's County: Yoknapatawpha* (Random House Publishers, 1963), *Life Magazine* and *Saturday Evening Post* from the 1930s and 1940s; and pictures in newspaper archives [e.g., the *Little Rock Gazette*] from Arkansas, 1930 to 1940; 2) a copy of *I Know Why the Caged Bird Sings*; 3) a copy of Maya Angelou's Inauguration Day poem for William Jefferson Clinton. It can be found in newspaper coverage of the Inauguration printed January 20-21, 1993. Ms. Angelou's poem is also available on audiotape.

Survivor

CONTEXT BUILDING: *Objectives*: 1) To help learners understand the experiences of Southeast Asian refugees who came to the United States in the 1970s; 2) to help learners who are studying English outside their own country realize that their own experiences of longing for their homeland and isolation in a foreign culture are shared by all refugees, immigrants, and international students.   **SUGGESTED MATERIALS:** 1) Pictures of Southeast Asian refugees escaping from Vietnam, being processed in refugee camps, and being settled in the United States. Good resources are Keith St. Cartmail, *Exodus Indochina* (Heineman Publishers, 1983); publications of the United Nations High Commission on Refugees (UNHCR) from the 1970s; and *Newsweek* and *Washington Post* news stories from June-July, 1979. Useful background reading for the instructor includes Paul S. Strand and Woodrow Jones, *Indochinese Refugees in America* (Duke University Press, 1985). 2) Related readings for ESL learners include *Tales from the Homeland* (Alemany Press); John Dennis O, *Promised Land* (Newbury House Publishers, 1982); and John Mundahl, *Tales of Courage* (Addison-Wesley Publishers, 1993). Relevant video presentations include Ken Levine and Ivory Waterworth Levine, *Becoming America* (New Day Films, Inc., 1980?); and Suzanne Griffin, Giles Baker, and Maxine Fang-Yi Loo, *Children of Change* (University of Washington, Instructional Media Services, 1983).

Going Home

CONTEXT BUILDING: *Objectives*: 1) To give learners a sense of the physical setting of this story: a Greyhound bus trip through the eastern United States; 2) to help learners understand the psychological state of a person who has been out of touch with society (e.g., a parolee from prison or a hostage) for a long time and is returning to an unceratin future; 3) to give learners an understanding of the emotions of those waiting for loved ones who have been forcibly kept away from them for a long time.   **SUGGESTED**

225

MATERIALS: 1) Pictures of long distance buses (e.g., Greyhound and Trailways) and bus stations in America; 2) stories and pictures by and about ex-convicts and individuals who were held hostage in foreign countries. Good resources include news stories and pictures about American hostages in Iran (*Newsweek* and *Time*, November 1979 and subsequent months); 3) stories and songs about loved ones waiting for the release of hostages, especially news stories about American hostage Terry Anderson's family from the 1980s and the song "Tie A Yellow Ribbon on the Old Oak Tree."

THE RED DOG

CONTEXT BUILDIN: *Objectives*: To help learners understand the attachment that frequently exists between Americans and their dogs. **SUGGESTED MATERIALS:** 1) Pictures of dogs and their owners, including a picture of an Irish setter; 2) pictures of dogs, including hunting dogs, in a country setting. Good resources: calenders with a dog theme, children's books, guides for pet owners.

UNIT 5: VISIONS

I HAVE A DREAM

CONTEXT BUILDING: *Objectives*: 1) To stimulate learners to see the parallel between the struggles for equality of minorities in their own countries and the struggles of African Americans in the United States; 2) to help learners understand the social context of the Civil Rights Movement and Martin Luther King's speech: the prejudice shown against African Americans by whites; 3) to give learners a better understanding of Martin Luther King, the man, the leader, and the orator. **SUGGESTED MATERIALS:** 1) The selection from Maya Angelou's *I Know Why the Caged Bird Sings* in Unit 4; 2) pictures and writings from the American Civil Rights Movement (see *Life Magazine* issues from the early 1960s); 3) writings by Martin Luther King; 4) newspaper stories on microfiche from August 28, 1963 (The MArch on Washington) and a recording of Martin Luther King's speech.

THE LAST NIGHT OF THE WORLD

CONTEXT BUILDING: *Objectives*: 1) To help learners understand cultural and religious differences in beliefs about the future of the world; 2) to help learners articulate what they value most in life by having them list the last things they would like to experience if the world were ending; 3) to help learners recognize the importance of routine in creating a sense of stability in our lives. **SUGGESTED MATERIALS:** Notecards or sheets of paper for personal lists and newsprint and markers for making class lists. **PROCESS:** 1) Students should make personal lists and share only what they wish to share when making a class list of the last things they would like to experience if the world were ending; 3) to help learners recognize the importance of routine in creating a sense of stability in our lives.

ACCEPTANCE SPEECH

CONTEXT BUILDING: *Objectives*: 1) To help learners recall events from their own lives which will help them understand the occassion of Faulkner's speech; 2) to help learners understand Faulkner's message by contrasting the lists of things that evoke fear with those that give hope; 3) to help learners relate their own belief system to Faulkner's belief in the triumph of the human spirit; 4) to help learners appreciate Faulkner's writing and the county about which he wrote. **SUGGESTED MATERIALS:** 1) Note cards for personal lists and newsprint and markers for class lists; 2) short stories and novels by William Faulkner and Martin Dain's *Faulkner's County: Yoknapatawpha* (Random House Publishers, 1963).

Answer Key

UNIT 1: FABLES OLD AND NEW

THE DONKEY IN THE LION'S SKIN
Exercise A: **1.** F **2.** T **3.** F **4.** T **5.** F **6.** T **7.** F **8.** T

Exercise B: **1.** students' sentences will vary **2. a.** the villagers, the donkey **b.** oxen and horses **c.** men, women, children, dogs, horses, cats, oxen, sheep, and pigs **d.** the donkey in the lion's skin **e.** the donkey in the lion's skin **f.** the donkey in the lion's skin **g.** his master led the donkey **h.** a fox

Exercise C: **1.** b (or a) **2.** c **3.** b and c **4.** a **5.** c

Exercise D: Part One: 1. run, get, give **3.** to escape, to leave very quickly **4.** give away is more final; you do not get something back if you give it away. In the context of this story, give away means reveal **5.** away = to another place, in a different direction **Part Two: a.** M **b.** M **c.** M **d.** G

THE MILKMAID AND HER PAIL
Exercise A: **1.** F **2.** F **3.** F **4.** T **5.** F **6.** T **7.** F **8.** F

Exercise B: **1.** students' sentences will vary **2. a.** the chicks **b.** the milkmaid ("I") **c.** everybody (Polly Shaw, Molly Parsons, Jack Squire) **d.** the milkmaid **e.** the milkmaid **3.** students' responses will vary

Exercise C: **1.** b **2.** a **3.** c **4.** b **5.** a

Exercise D: Part One: 1i. all the eggs, all the milk, walked past them all, nothing at all to sell, all her fine dreams, all her friends (choose 5) **1ii.** Yes **1iii.** No **2.** different **3. a.** He lost all his money. **b.** I like all your friends. **c.** She had nothing at all to say. **d.** John got all his answers correct. **e.** Bill didn't understand the question at all. **Part Two: i.** 10 times **iii.** "I will look fine. . . ." etc. **iv.** Question word — "Won't" adds emphasis. **v.** The opposite. *Please* come in = *Won't you* come in.

THE BONFIRE AND THE ANTS
Exercise A: **1.** F **2.** F **3.** T **4.** T **5.** F **6.** F **7.** T

Exercise B: **1.** students' sentences will vary **2. a.** the writer **b.** the writer **c.** the ants **d.** "Their" might apply to refugees or immigrants

Exercise C: **1.** b **2.** b **3.** c **4.** c **5.** b, c, a **6.** a **7.** b

Exercise D: **1.** notice **2.** scurried **3.** managed to **4.** perished **5.** forsaken **6.** gripped **7.** overcame

Exercise E: *Matching exercise* **1.** k **2.** b **3.** d, e **4.** j, a, h **5.** a, l **6.** c **7.** l, k **8.** h **9.** a, g, k **10.** i **11.** f

THE UNICORN IN THE GARDEN
Exercise A: **1.** T **2.** F **3.** F **4.** T **5.** T **6.** T **7.** T **8.** F

Exercise B: **1.** students' sentences will vary **2. a.** the man (husband) **b.** the wife **c.** the unicorn **d.** the wife talking to the husband **e.** the man (husband) **f.** the wife **g.** the police and the psychiatrist looked at the wife **h.** the police **i.** the police were subduing the wife **j.** the police talking about the wife

Exercise C: **1.** b **2.** a, b **3.** a, c **4.** c **5.** b **6.** c **7.** b

Exercise D: students' reponses will vary

Exercise E: **4.** The story has a "choppy" or "sing-song" quality because of the short, unconnected sentences. The story moves less easily after you remove the *ands*.

UNIT 2: SORROWS

A WHITE MAN'S WORD
Exercise A: **1.** T **2.** F **3.** F **4.** T **5.** F **6.** T **7.** F **8.** F **9.** F

Exercise B: **1.** students' sentences will vary **2. a.** the writer's son **b.** white children in the pool **c.** the narrator (Debi) thinking about her friend and her friend's mom **d.** one of the eight-year-old white girls speaking to her friend **e.** Daddy (the narrator's father)

f. Native Americans as described by one of the eight-year-old white girls g. Debi's friend's mom h. Debi's father speaking to her, and eighteen years later, Debi speaking to her son

Exercise C: 1. c 2. a 3. b 4. c 5. c 6. d

Exercsie D: brown; pale; black (or dark); sure; unafraid; noticeable; remain (or stay); bright, new (or modern); wavy (or curly); light, thin; carelessly; white (or Caucasian)

THE GEESE

Exercise A: 1. F 2. F 3. T 4. F 5. T 6. T 7. F

Exercise B: 1. students' sentences will vary 2. a. Liz (the goose who was Apathy's sister b. the old gander c. Apathy d. the author/narrator who lived on the farm e. the young gander attacking the old gander f. three swallows circling overhead g. the young gander h. the old gander i. the old gander sitting in the sun is compared to old men sitting on benches

Exercise C: 1. b 2. b 3. b 4. b 5. d

Exercise D: a. young and old ganders b. young gander c. young and old ganders d. young and old ganders e. old gander f. young gander g. Liz h. Apathy i. old gander j. five goslings k. the narrator l. Apathy m. old gander n. young gander o. five goslings p. narrator q. narrator r. old gander s. narrator t. goslings The ganders receive most of the description because the author's purpose is to focus on their struggle and his own feelings about the old gander's defeat.

THANK YOU MA'M

Exercise A: 1. T 2. F 3. F 4. T 5. F 6. F 7. F 8. T 9. F 10. T

Exercise B: 1. students' sentences will vary 2. a. a large woman (Luella Bates Washington Jones) b. Mrs. Jones speaking to the boy c. the boy speaking to Mrs. Jones d. Mrs. Jones speaking to the boy e. the boy asking Mrs. Jones f. Mrs. Jones speaking to the boy g. the boy thinking about what he wanted to do h. Mrs. Jones reflecting on her own life i. Mrs. Jones j. the boy

Exercsie C: 1. b 2. c 3. b 4. b, d, c, a 5. c 6. b (or a) 7. c 8. c 9. c 10. c

Exercise D: Part One: 1. have 2. have 3. must (have to) 4. buy 5. obtain or buy 6. be able to 7. becoming 8. receive 9. buy or obtain 10. received **Part Two:** (students' answers may vary) 1. to buy a pair of shoes (1) 2. to wash his face (2) 3. to pick Roger up (2) 4. to look (2) 5. to wash his face (2) 6. to clean up; to wash his face (2) 7. to heat up some food (2)

Exercise E: Part One: 1. e 2. d 3. a 4. c 5. b 6. g 7. f **Part Two: 1.** Don't you have anybody at home? **2.** As late as it is . . **3.** Maybe you haven't had your supper. **4.** I was young once. **5.** You are going to remember me. **6.** He doesn't know any better. **7.** We are going to eat dinner now.

YOU GO YOUR WAY, I'LL GO MINE

Exercise A: 1. T 2. F 3. F 4. T 5. F 6. T 7. T 8. F 9. T 10. F

Exercise B: 1. students' sentences will vary 2. a. Homer waiting for the woman to answer the door b. Mrs. Sandoval, upon opening the door and seeing Homer c. Homer, thinking about the news in the telegram d. Mrs. Sandoval, explaining that she only reads Spanish e. Mrs. Sandoval's question to Homer f. the workers in the War Department g. Mrs. Sandoval to Homer, who is reluctant to come into her house h. Mrs. Sandoval to Homer i. Homer, while sitting and watching Mrs. Sandoval cry j. Homer, explaining to himself that he did not cause the death of Juan Domingo

Exercise C: 1. b 2. a 3. a 4. b 5. a 6. c 7. b 8. c, d, a 9. a

Exercsie D: Part One: 1. feel 2. opened 3. study 4. say 5. studied 6. made 7. felt 8. make 9. open 10. say 11. open 12. made 13. opened or felt 14. studied 15. felt **Part Two: a.** bring **b.** to pick up **c.** to smooth out **d.** bring **e.** to tell **f.** must **g.** to chew **h.** would **i.** to do, could **j.** to take

UNIT 3: MEMORIES

ANTONIO'S FIRST DAY OF SCHOOL

Exercise A: 1. T 2. F 3. F 4. T 5. F 6. T 7. F 8. T 9. T 10. F

Exercise B: 1. students' sentences will vary 2. **a.** Antonio **b.** the school building **c.** the red-haired boy **d.** the school building **e.** the red-haired boy led Antonio **f.** Miss Maestro asking Antonio a question **g.** non-Hispanic children **h.** the other children (non-Hispanic Americans) **i.** Mother **j.** Antonio

Exercise C: 1. b 2. c 3. a 4. a 5. b 6. b 7. a 8. b 9. c 10. a

Exercise D: white-legged, brown-skinned, red-faced, thin-fingered, long-footed, thick-lipped, weak-handed, fat-armed, left-hipped, black-haired Other combinations that are semantically sensible should be accepted.

Exercise E: (some possibe answers) **1.** "I awoke with a sick feeling in my stomach." **2.** "A huge lump seemed to form in my throat and tears came to my eyes." **3.** "I yearned for my mother and at the same time I understood that she had sent me to this place where I was an outcast." **4.** "The other boys and girls laughed and pointed at me." **or** "They showed me their sandwiches which were made of bread." **5.** "I kept away from the group as much as I could and worked alone." **6.** "We found a few others who were like us, different in language and customs, and a part of our loneliness was gone." **or** "We bonded together and in our union found strength."

George Washington, My Countryman

Exercise A: 1. T 2. F 3. T 4. F 5. F 6. F 7. F 8. T

Exercise B: 1. students' sentences will vary 2. **a.** Mary Antin **b.** George Washington **c.** Jews **d.** Mary Antin's fathers reacting to her poem **e.** Miss Dwight, Mary's teacher **f.** Geoge Washington **g.** the editor of the *Boston Transcript* **h.** the editor of the *Boston Herald* **i.** thousands of people (readers of the *Boston Herald*) **j.** Mary's father

Exercise C: 1. d 2. c 3. a 4. c 5. d 6. d 7. c

Exercise D: Part One: 2. tremble — body; embrace — arms; point — finger; cry — eyes; twitch — neck or eyelid; stare — eyes; bend — back, arms, legs; turn —legs; shrug — shoulders; touch — hands; yell — mouth; knock — hand Other combinations that are semantically sensible should be accepted. **Part Two:** students' responses will vary

Chinese School

Exercise A: 1. F 2. F 3. T 4. T 5. F 6. T 7. T 8. T 9. T 10. T 11. F

Exercise B: 1. students' sentences will vary 2. **a.** The Chinses teachers put the author in a low level class **b.** the Chinese teacher **c.** the Chinese teacher **d.** the author **e.** the Chinese teacher **f.** author being addressed by the teacher **g.** the author explaining why she couldn't write **h.** the other kids **i.** the author being addressed by the teacher **j.** the author generalizing her experience

Exercise C: 1. c 2. a 3. a 4. b 5. b 6. a 7. b, c

Exercise D: Students' responses will vary.

Music Lady

Exercise A: 1. T 2. F 3. T 4. T 5. T 6. F 7. F

Exercise B: 1. students' sentences will vary 2. **a.** the record store **b.** the listening booths **c.** Bach **d.** the author as she stood outside a listening booth **e.** the owner **f.** grownups **g.** Mrs. Smith as an old woman **h.** the author, upon seeing Mrs. Smith after many years **i.** the author told Mrs. Smith about her kindness years before

Exercise C: sample answers 1. it had listening booths; the author was there 2. Big Band music; tribal music 3. helped her to compose poetry 4. she appreciated the author's love of poetry and music 5. thanked Mrs. Smith for her kindness and encouragement

Exercise D: sample answers 1. running so fast her legs and chest hurt 2. the bins or containers that held the records, which had the faces of the musicians on the covers 3. wonderful music that could be heard through the doors of the listening booths 4. the way the author described herself 5. I nodded "yes" 6. This kind of music reminded her of her mother 7. Mrs Smith was old 8. she held the record gently between her hands

UNIT 4: TIES

I Know Why the Caged Bird Sings

Exercise A: 1. F 2. T 3. F 4. T 5. T 6. F 7. T 8. F 9. T 10. T

Exercise B: **1.** students' sentences will vary **2. a.** the "Negro" **b.** white people **c.** Uncle Willie **d.** Maya and Bailey **e.** the African American population **f.** Maya and Bailey **g.** Maya's mother (as she imagined her) **h.** Bailey, Maya's brother **i.** Maya and Bailey **j.** Maya

Exercise C: **1.** b **2.** c **3.** b **4.** a **5.** a **6.** a

Exercsie D: **1.** g, or a with *but* **2.** a, c, e, g with *but*; b or f with *so* **3.** a, c, e, g with *but*; b with *so* **4.** d, g, with *but* **5.** a, c, with *but*; d, f with *and* or *so* **6.** e, g with *but*; b, f with *so* **7.** c, f with *but*

Exercsie E: **1.** money and discriminating practices against African Americans **2.** that they were in a Depression **3.** everyone was poorer — the Depression did not discriminate **4.** because they never heard from them **5.** because they realized that their parents were alive and still didn't want to have them live with them **6.** because they had done something wrong **7.** she was glad her parents weren't dead but upset that her mother and father would live happily in California without their children **8.** Their parents might come riding up. They should be ready and keep the tea set in good condition. **9.** because they were hurt and angry

THE RED DOG

Exercise A: **1.** F **2.** F **3.** T **4.** T **5.** F **6.** T **7.** T **8.** F **9.** T **10.** F

Exercise B: **1.** students' sentences will vary **2. a.** Spook **b.** the author, deciding what to do with Spook when he went to war **c.** the author wondered if his friend, the owner of the local garage, would take care of Spook and love him **d.** the author wrote his friends in the village to ask for news about Spook **e.** the author's friend, owner of the local garage **f.** the author told Laurette the story about Spook having been passed from one master in the valley to another **g.** Spook, when the author saw him in the pasture **h.** Spook, encountering his former owner for the first time on four years **i.** Spook's signs of remembering his first master **j.** the Crocker boy — Spook's current master **k.** Laurette, prior to pleading with the author to stop the car because Spook has chased their speeding car down the road **l.** the author, talking to Laurette about her change of mind over what to do with Spook **m.** the author, referring to his nightmare about Spook chasing his car and feeling unwanted by his master

Exercise C: **1.** c **2.** b **3.** a **4.** b **5.** b **6.** a **7.** c **8.** b **9.** a **10.** c

Exercise D: **i.** Spook had a deep red mahognay coat (1) **ii.** "He was a king." (1) "Spook quartered the field, racing far ahead and then back again." (16) **iii.** "All the way up in the car he had watched me." (5) "He stood there looking into my face for a minute — then — without a bark or wag of his tail — curled up on the stone at my feet . . . he watched every move I made . . ." (19) **See paragraphs 1, 16, 18-24, 30-34**

Exercsie E: **1.** Looking in the window, he saw a dog. **2.** Waiting for a bus, she ran into an old friend. **3.** Padding into the restaurant, the dog appeared healthy. **4.** Leaving the supermarket, Tom glanced at the garage across the street. **5.** Looking at the dog, he felt very sad. **6.** Glancing in the rear-view mirror, he saw Spook running his heart out. **7.** Hearing a sound from the car, I turned around. **8.** Talking to him, I explained what happened. **9.** Patting her shoulder, I gave her my handkerchief. (or, Giving her my handkerchief . . .) **10.** Waking up in a cold sweat, I slip quietly out of bed.

SURVIVOR

Part I: Exercise A: **1.** F **2.** F **3.** F **4.** F **5.** F **6.** T **7.** T **8.** F **9.** T **10.** F

Exercise B: **1.** c **2.** a, c, d, e **3.** a **4.** a **5.** a

Part II: Exercise A: **1.** F **2.** T **3.** F **4.** F **5.** F **6.** F **7.** T **8.** F

Exercise B: **1.** b, c **2.** a **3.** b **4.** a **5.** c **6.** d

Exercise C: **1.** students' sentences will vary **2. a.** Mrs Kincaid, the apartment manager **b.** Thi Nham Binh speaking about her illness as a spiritual one, caused by a broken heart **c.** Thi Nham Binh speaking to Mrs. Green **d.** Thi Nham Binh's father **e.** *you* Americans **f.** Thi Nham Binh's mother offered her jewelry to Quang, the boatman **g.** the Vietnamese refugees on the sailboat **h.** the Catholic Relief Agency on Java **i.** Thi Nham Binh's relative (her mother's nephew) **j.** Miss Green speaking to Thi Nham Binh

Exercise D: **1.** b **2.** d **3.** f **4.** a **5.** i **6.** c **7.** h **8.** j **9.** e **10.** g

Going Home

Exercise A: 1. T 2. T 3. F 4. F 5. F 6. T 7. F 8. F 9. T 10. F 11. T 12. T

Exercise B: 1. students' sentences will vary 2. a. the young people from New York who were on the bus to Fort Lauderdale b. Vingo c. Vingo — one of the speculations about him by the young people d. the girl conversing with Vingo about Florida e. Vingo f. Vingo's wife g. the girl's question to Vingo h. Vingo reporting his message to his wife i. the young people j. the old con (Vingo)

Exercise C: 1. a 2. b 3. b 4. a 5. b 6. c 7. b 8. c 9. a 10. b

Exercise D: 1. "Are you going that far?" 2. "Do you live there?" 3. "Do you want some wine?" 4. "And she didn't write to you for three and a half years?" 5. If she didn't want me, she should not tie a handkerchief to the tree.

Exercise E: 1. When Vingo . . . , he sat . . . 2. Because Vingo . . . , he had been in jail . . . 3. When the bus . . . , everybody . . . 4. When the bus stopped, . . . the old con . . . 5. If she wants me . . . , she should tie . . . 6. When (as soon as) the young people . . . , one of the girls . . . 7. Because he was preparing . . . Vingo tightened . . . 8. As they got on . . . , they were carrying . . . 9. While Vingo told . . . , he showed . . . **The correct order of events is:** 2, 8, 3, 6, 9, 5, 7, 1, 4

UNIT 5: VISIONS

I Have A Dream

Exercise A: 1. F 2. F 3. T 4. F 5. T 6. T 7. F 8. F 9. T 10. T

Exercise B: 1. students' sentences will vary 2. a. America b. descendants of slaves (African Americans) and descendants of slaveholders (Southern white Americans) c. Mississippi d. Martin Luther King's children e. all human beings

Exercise C: 1. c 2. b 3. c 4. b 5. b 6. b 7. c 8. b 9. b 10. c 11. a 12. a

Exercise D: 1. d 2. e 3. a 4. c 5. b

Exercise E: 1. Maria told her mother (that) she liked . . . 2. MLK told him (that) his . . . 3. I have a feeling (that) many people . . . 4. He hopes (that) someday he will be . . . 5. Do you think (that) the Civil Rights Movement was successful? 6. Many people believe (that) MLK was a great men. 7. Did you know (that) MLK was assassinated? 8. He believes (that) non-violent . . .

The Last Night of the World

Exercise A: 1. F 2. F 3. T 4. F 5. T 6. F 7. T 8. F 9. T 10. F

Exercise B: 1. students' sentences will vary 2. a. the woman responding to her husband's question about the end of the world b. the husband speaking to his wife about his feelings when he contemplates the end of the world c. the voice in the dream the man had speaking about events on earth d. Stan Willis, the husband's office mate at work e. the wife's question to her husband about the end of the world f. the women on the block g. everyone h. the girls (daughters of the man and woman) i. other people j. the husband and wife

Exercise C: 1. b 2. b 3. b 4. d 5. b 6. c 7. a

Exercise D: Part I: 1. enormously 2. block 3. caught 4. background, playing 5. means 6. miss 7. touch 8. spirit 9. hell 10. poured 11. struck 12. blocks
Part II: 1. spirit 2. caught 3. poured 4. means 5. miss 6. struck 7. hell 8. played 9. background 10. blocked 11. touched 12. enormous

Exercise E: (sample answers, students' responses will vary) 1. He glanced at the girls and their yellow hair was shining in the lamplight. 2. There was an easy, clean aroma of the brewed coffee in the evening air. 3. . . . lay in their cool bed, their hands clasped, their heads together. 4. all of paragraph 4 5. . . . they lifted (the coffee) slowly and drank.

Nobel Prize Acceptance Speech

Exercise A: 1. students' responses may vary

Exercise B: 1. students' sentences will vary 2. a. award b. young male and female writers c. the question that people are worried about at the time; it's society's tragedy, according to Faulkner d. problems of the human heart in conflict e. a young writer (meaning **all** young writers, male and female) f. the poet, the writer

Credits